S0-BFB-300

Take
Five

Take Five

Steven Mosley

Pacific Press Publishing Association
Boise, Idaho
Oshawa, Ontario, Canada

Edited by Don Mansell
Designed by Tim Larson
Cover by Francis Livingston
Type set in 10/12 Century Schoolbook

All texts quoted in this book are from the New International Version unless otherwise indicated.

Copyright © 1987 by
Pacific Press Publishing Association
Printed in United States of America
All Rights Reserved

Library of Congress Catalog Card Number: 87-81983

ISBN 0-8163-0752-0

87 88 89 90 91 • 5 4 3 2 1

Dedicated to
Kaz, my favorite
picture of God's love

With deep roots and firm foundations, may you be strong to grasp, with all God's people, what is the breadth and length and height and depth of the love of Christ, and to know it, though it is beyond knowledge. So may you attain to fullness of being, the fullness of God himself. Ephesians 3:18, 19 NEB.

Contents

Introduction

I once heard a minister lamenting the fact that so few people had come to hear his message on the love of God. "If I had announced my topic as 'Satanism Today,' " he said, "this auditorium would probably be packed."

I wondered, too, why so many of us are more fascinated by the devil than by lofty truths like God's love. But then the preacher answered my question for me. He launched into an orderly, abstract exposition of the components of God's love A, B, C. I realized that if the sermon had been centered on Satan we would have heard about furniture levitating, the deceased reappearing, and people writhing on the floor—not the components of Satanism A, B, and C. We would have heard about Satan's eye-opening actions, not abstractions about him.

This book attempts to present a few of God's eye-opening actions—exploits that have opened my eyes to His many-faceted love. They are, for me, the moral equivalent of furniture levitating and the deceased reappearing. These experiences have formed in my life vivid pictures of God's ingenious and sometimes dramatic compassion—a gallery of His love.

A very present help in trouble.

Chapter 1

Take Five

Haruo leans forward, pressing his point home. "You wonder how I can believe in all this intangible religious stuff? Well, what if I told you there are private detectives and Samurai battles, Hawaiian beaches and lovers' dialogues floating around in our room right now? You would find that hard to believe too, wouldn't you?"

Seigi nods.

Haruo reaches over and turns on the television. "But it's true. I can't sense the dots of color that float into this TV set, but I can tell by the results I see that something invisible is acting on the television.

"It's the same with God. He can be known by His actions. At first, I found the talk about angels and God's Spirit living in people pretty odd too. But I've seen the results in people's lives."

Cut. Great!

Haruo and Seigi were doing a good job of acting out the parts of a new Christian and his skeptical friend. They had become accustomed to the heat of 2500 watts and the purring of my Super-8 camera. And Kazko, the Bible teacher who translated my scripts, was coaching the two young men well.

The movie, entitled *Seedling*, was one in a series I had been making for a Christian English school in Japan. The students there had many questions about the God we call Creator and Father. Little in their background had prepared them to understand an infinite, personal Deity. Instead of the Answer to life's questions, God, to them, was something of a mystifying stranger. The film was an attempt to show our students that God is active and knowable. I was also hoping it would help solidify the faith of Haruo and Seigi, both new believers.

Seedling, like my other films, was no Hollywood production. I had to make do with a small budget, miscellaneous equipment, and lots of could-you-spare-a-few-minutes.

This was to be our last night of filming. The camera had to be back in another city the following day, so we were trying to squeeze in the final retakes.

If only once, just once, I could set up a scene without being in a hurry. Makeshift movie making, it seems, always must be done on the fly—with antsy volunteers. In college I had a phenomenally patient roommate who let me spend hours composing shots of him walking down the sidewalk. But now when it really counted—the pressure never let up.

One of Seigi's lines wasn't recorded properly last week. We set things up to shoot him in a close-up. He sits behind a low table looking over the script. The lights are adjusted to lose his shadow on the wall. Camera and mike are ready. We roll. Seigi does his line pretty naturally, considering it's cut off from the rest of the dialogue.

But the camera sputters and skips. Groan. I check all the wires, battery light, batteries, switch, and lock—everything seems OK. I shake the film cartridge.

Lights. Second take. Seigi is into his line, but the camera still rattles unevenly. Please, not now... Just a few little pickup shots to finish the film, and what happens? Disgusted and desperate I take out the old batteries, which are working, and insert a new set into the camera grip.

Lights. Take three. Brand-name X camera still stutters. Gnash. Gnash. "OK," I tell Seigi, "Let me roll about ten feet of film in case something is jammed in the cartridge." For some reason I put the old batteries back in.

Lights again please. Take four. I squeeze the switch with great intensity, as if that could help, and shoot about a minute of film. Nothing clears. The camera sputters on, doggedly erratic.

My head in hot and blank. I stare at my little black camera, completely flustered. There are no more switches or cables to fiddle with.

Then Kazko makes a suggestion. "Let's pray about it."

Oh yes, prayer. I've been too busy wrestling with the problem to think of that. Fortunately Kazko sees God's opportunity.

So the four of us kneel together, tell the Lord of our genuine need, and put our trust in His abilities.

We finish praying and look at each other for a moment. I stare at the recalcitrant camera. There's nothing more anyone can do.

Take five. Action. The camera makes such a melodious purr in my ear that I barely hear Seigi's line. The chronic sputtering is gone! We're all shouting together, slapping each other on the back.

We shot without a hitch the rest of the evening and completed the film. I was anxious to see our last roll. As soon as the footage came back from the lab I projected Seigi's one-line pickup. The picture frame jumped and skipped during the first four takes; the sound was out of sync too. On the fifth take, picture and sound were perfect.

I rushed off to tell Haruo, Seigi, and Kazko. Our film project was finally completed. We rejoiced together. But it wasn't the successful filming that excited us so much as the feeling that we had seen our Lord come by, very close. He had appeared, not just in someone's cloudy vision, but in the mechanical innards of a movie camera. Haruo and Seigi had a new light in their eyes. God had acted. So much for intangible religious stuff.

God flooded our inmost heart.

—Romans 5:5, NEB.

Chapter 2

From Tulsa, With Grace

Just inside the vestibule we peered cautiously at the long pews and smattering of saints, not at all sure that our faded jeans and unkempt hair would find a welcome. After all, this was Tulsa, Oklahoma, where the solid folk croon along with, "Proud to be an Okie from Muskogee." But the Baptist chapel seemed to be our only alternative.

Soon an elderly woman came over and invited us to sit down for "Reverend Johnson's talk." We scooted into a pew at the back of the small church and listened to the reverend deliver his Sunday vesper message. He spoke with simple, unadorned conviction. Behind him, on the bare, white wall, hung a tiny picture of Jesus.

After smiling our way through greetings at the end of the service, we explained our problem. On the way back from a summer Christian training conference in Dallas, our bus had broken down and was towed to a filling station nearby. Most of the youth had taken a Greyhound home. Five of us had decided to stay and try to get the bus fixed. We had discovered too late that the mechanics at the gas station were dishonest.

The church folk were eager to help. Especially a Mr. John Reed who had a mechanic friend. "Why we'll have 'er runnin' in no time," he said cheerfully. "Ralph can fix most anything."

After a phone call, Ralph, the mechanic, came by and opened up the hood. Mark, the other driver, and I tried in vain to recall meaningful symptoms for him. "Well we were driving along the highway and . . . it quit . . . it just died."

17

Ralph climbed into our venerable yellow school bus and turned on the ignition key. The engine responded with a token groan. After Ralph poked around under the bus for a while, it became obvious that our vehicle wouldn't be fixed that night. But Mr. Reed—slightly balding, open-faced and freckled—had an idea. "Listen, you all can come over and stay at our house. We've got plenty of room. We'll get this thing goin' in the morning."

We couldn't come up with any of the polite refusals that customarily keep strangers from barging in. There was just our suddenly retired bus and the empty night. So we gratefully climbed into Mr. Reed's 1961 station wagon.

In their suburban home, the Reeds made room. Their house had seen a lot of living and showed no traces of luxury, but in some mysterious way Mr. Reed and his wife made the thought that we were imposing evaporate from our minds. It was like we were their kids home from college. A sofa here, a few cots on the screened porch there, and everyone was settled.

It took a good part of the next day to find engine parts. Joe drove us around, pointing out the "sights" of Tulsa. Other men from the church came in the evening. They joked together, took Mrs. Reed's hot drink, and installed the parts, while we collegiates stood around feigning assistance. Finally, our bus started in earnest. The men cheered, had a final cup, and departed into the night.

Tuesday morning, after a savory meal of biscuits, scrambled eggs, and grits, we boarded our purring vehicle and thanked the Reeds profusely. We had nothing to offer but thanks. They had provided everything else. As Janet, the lone girl in our group, cried half-cheerfully, we waved from the windows and pulled out.

After a couple of miles through the suburbs our bus began to screech—horrible noises, as if the motor had turned on itself. The clatter reverberated from different places, cleverly disguising the source of the problem. Mark and I jumped out and opened the hood. We stared at the engine for what seemed a respectfully long enough time, poking around, commenting sagely to each other—"Yeah that's the radiator all right."

Pulling up noisily at the now familiar blue frame house, we smiled sheepishly at John Reed, "It started making awful noises."

This time it took two days to fix. But the Reeds remained gracious—"Great, you kids can come to prayer meeting with us."

At the little Tulsa chapel a warbling organ cranked out hymns that I had always thought rather dull. But that night, singing among those square jaws and weathered faces, I caught a new warmth from the old familiar phrases.

Reverend Johnson asked us if we would get up and "testify" about the Lord's blessing at our conference. The five of us went up to the creaky wooden platform one by one and told of what we'd learned, of our witnessing experiences, and of the excitement of being with thousands of others praising the Lord together.

John and Evelyn beamed at us proudly as we mumbled out our words of witness. They looked for all the world like proud parents at a graduation.

Afterwards, everyone enthusiastically thanked us. We had said so little. But they called it a "wonderful blessing." Our "Okie" friends felt like their small, isolated congregation was now bound to the larger body of Christ.

Thursday morning. Another tearful farewell. Our bus lumbered along amiably for an entire two blocks before falling fast asleep in third gear. It couldn't be coaxed awake. A highway patrolman dropped by. We tried to explain that friends down the road could help us in just a few minutes. But he insisted that our bus had to be towed off the narrow road immediately.

So near and yet so far. The patrolman radioed a truck and we were towed across town to "Ace Garage," its gravel lot conspicuously full of police cars.

I got on the phone. "John, it's me again."

"Well I'll be switched. How far did you all get this time?" John wasn't upset. His voice sounded as affable as ever. "You sit tight, hear? We'll be over in a jiffy."

We managed to revive the bus enough for it to crawl back to the Reeds' home, and wait for Ralph to come in the evening.

The five of us feasted on green beans, corn-on-the-cob, and

other delicacies. In the afternoon, Janet looked at old photo albums with Evelyn; Mark and Sydney helped John touch up the front siding; and Fred and I helped Jerry Reed, age twelve, feed his rabbits in the backyard. It felt good to be just family.

Friday morning. "This is going to be it," we said confidently. We again waved to "Mom" and "Papa" Reed through the bus windows. They stood for a long time on their narrow crabgrass lawn.

We got to the outskirts of Tulsa before our crotchety, yellow vehicle started hinting. Little groans here and there. All was not well. The motor misfired. The hinting grew more persistent. Mark and I grimaced at each other.

Finally, we decided to turn around. There was no way we could make it to Illinois. All of us wondered what the Reeds would say this, the third time. Surely they wouldn't believe it; surely we'd catch a hint of tension in their faces. But no, "Papa" was out on the lawn waving as soon as our telltale sputtering could be heard coming up "Farswell Drive."

We apologized lamely. John wouldn't hear of it, "Glad to have you back."

During our entire stay in Tulsa we never saw a trace of the wearying strain that must come from having five extra people camp out in your home. The Reeds' welcome was tested to the limit but it never flinched.

One guy in our group, Fred, was black. The neighbors imperfectly concealed their distress about his sleeping in their midst. But John told me it didn't matter to him. He was proud to be sheltering the youth.

We had popped out of the alien ambiance of protesting, drug-infested universities into their Okie land of country music and the flag. Yet our two mutually intangible worlds presented no barriers. Mom and Papa Reed always treated us as a special blessing. They valued us for our fellowship and accepted us, extra toothbrushes, sleeping bags, dirty socks and all.

Sabbath arrived—our fourth attempt at departure. The five of us embraced our adopted family and said hopeful, sad good-byes. This time Janet's tears were not shed in vain. We held the road all the way home to Illinois.

As meaningful as that experience was in my life, it was one more final meeting that crystallized for me the unique worth of my Tulsa friends.

The following Christmas, my family took a trip south to Texas. We were passing by Tulsa on a Sunday when I suddenly remembered the chapel close by the freeway and talked my parents into stopping for a few minutes.

The worship service was almost over when I stepped inside. Reverend Johnson spoke of the same verities with the same conviction. During the closing hymn we exchanged excited glances across the pews.

Outside, under a noon-high sun, their happiness rushed over me. I don't think I knew what it meant to be greeted before then. They were overjoyed to see me again, so glad I had dropped in. Papa Reed kept telling my dumfounded parents what a tremendous boon I and the others had been to their church.

Those people's delight just because I was present, struck at something marrow-deep in me. John's youngest, a seven-year-old, had been away at summer camp during the broken-down-bus episode. The girl had never laid eyes on me before, but rushed over anyway and hugged my waist earnestly as if for a long-lost brother. At that moment I felt I was poured into being. All the marketable qualities that I unconsciously relied on to make me feel valuable—the with-it clothes, the clever lines, the flashy personality—all seemed insignificant and were brushed aside in the warmth of the moment. I had nothing with which to recommend myself. I became empty, illuminatingly so, and in that sudden vacuum, experienced the grace of being poured full by their heady jubilation.

I suppose some would write off that church as no spiritual powerhouse. From the inside it may even have felt rather dry. Sunday by Sunday the believers gave their sincere but drowsy assent to the sermon. A casual visitor would probably catch little excitement from the group. Yet a potent love simmered in that aged stone building squatting diffidently by the rush of interstaters. That congregation disclosed "the grace of the Lord Jesus Christ" to me, banners blowing.

I have been inspired by many accounts of the bountiful grace of the Father. But before that encounter in Tulsa I don't think I ever truly knew it for the tangible, fundamental force that it is. Before, it was an area of theology on paper, a word constantly in search of a definition. In Tulsa I met it head on—a grace that filled me to the brim.

Are not sparrows two a penny? Yet without your Father's leave not one of them can fall to the ground.

—Matthew 10:29, NEB.

Chapter 3

Alan's Answer

Herding eight feisty adolescents through the routine of morning inspection, craft classes, kitchen duty, and campfire took all the energy and patience I could muster. Sometimes it took more. It was a constant struggle to preserve a semblance of order in my explosive little troop of campers that summer at Little Grassy Lake Camp.

I worked as a cabin counselor. Used to just hanging out with other college kids, I was very unfamiliar with the challenge of "mothering" squirmy urchins. But our goals were clear. We were supposed to make Christ real to these boys, many of whom had grown up with only a vaguely forbidding religious presence in their homes.

Each morning before breakfast all the campers filed out of their cabins toward the parade ground for a short worship. The camp director, standing tall in his immaculate uniform, usually gave a short talk on some Christian virtue. Then we divided by cabins into prayer groups.

Most of the kids in my circle bowed their heads, shuffled their feet, and mumbled a few words of greeting at the Almighty. They weren't that well acquainted with Him, but, having been persuaded that reverence was the better part of valor, figured it was the decent thing to do—all except Alan, that is. He stood up straight, arms folded, communicating his disapproval of the whole affair. Every morning it was the same. Something about petitioning the Lord bothered Alan. He always glanced around impatiently and tried to look as bored as possible as the rest bowed their heads.

I wanted to find out what could have made him dislike religion so early in life, but Alan was aloof. A ten-year-old strong-and-silent type. On occasion I could get him to talk about his trail rides on the camp minibikes, but he showed enthusiasm for little else.

One day during free period our group was out practicing for a softball game. The boys were lined up in the outfield catching flies. I smacked one over Alan's head into some bushes behind right field. He couldn't come up with the ball, so I ran out to help him look. We searched through the undergrowth for several minutes, but couldn't spot it.

Then I realized this might be a golden opportunity. "Hey, Alan," I suggested, "let's pray and see if God can help us find the ball." He responded with a languid, "OK."

Alan bowed his head ever so slightly this time, and I said a short prayer. We turned for another look through the bushes and quickly came up with the lost ball. I tried to get Alan excited: "Hey that was great; God really helped us find it." The boy was glad we could go on with our practice, but I wasn't sure whether our "luck" in retrieving the softball really sank in. The incident seemed quickly forgotten.

The next day at lunch I found myself with a few moments of peace and quiet after my kids had raced off to their swimming classes. It was nice to be able to eat without simultaneously acting as referee, janitor, and crisis-prevention expert.

As I lingered over my spaghetti, Alan came rushing up to the table, his face animated with an uncharacteristic excitement. "Guess what," he burst out, "I got my swimming honor. We took our test today. I prayed that God would help me, and I did good. He really helped me. The teacher said I did good." Alan proudly showed me his signed certificate.

I pounded the boy on the back and congratulated him on his successful collaboration with the Lord—trying not to show my surprise. I hadn't expected Alan to take up the challenge of prayer so quickly. As a matter of fact, I really hadn't expected it at all. Now his eyes sparkled with a great discovery.

I spent the last two days of camp in the infirmary, down with the flu, wondering what was happening with the kids. Just before boarding the bus home they came in to say goodbye. Alan was beaming. The previous night at a special campfire he had responded to the camp chaplain's invitation to accept Christ. "And I'm going to be baptized, too, as soon as I get home," he announced excitedly.

After the buses rumbled off and left the camp strangely quiet, I thought a lot about Alan and his joyful Yes to God. I wondered how, at first, this little kid filtered out so completely all our recommendations of God's goodness and love. Perhaps it was because we made them cloudy abstractions drifting far above him. But I was very, very thankful at that moment that God's love does reach down to earth. It touches down concretely—a softball lost in the underbrush, a child's thrashing limbs in a swimming pool.

The Lord disciplines those whom he loves.

—Hebrews 12:6, NEB.

Chapter 4

Right Between the Eyes

Would you believe it? Here it is 11:00 p.m. and Joe's still out goofing off. And he was supposed to be so tired he couldn't make it through the last of his English drills tonight. Some teacher. The guy's already four lessons behind. There's NO excuse for that. (Lord help me love Joe.) He's always late for staff meetings and then has to read letters when we're trying to get things done. I wonder if Joe is really here or back in California with the "cutesy-pie" he spends all his time writing to.

These thoughts blustered through me as I lay, trying to sleep, in the August humidity of Osaka, Japan. I was in my second year as a student missionary, teaching Bible and English at a language school. My roommates were still adjusting to the challenge of communicating their faith in an unfamiliar culture. I had come to think of myself as a wise veteran who had to put up with the cultural illiteracy of newcomers.

It seemed that every new crop of college kids expended their greatest energies in the pursuit of cameras, tape recorders, and tourist attractions. Where was their spirit of selfless dedication?

And Joe was the quintessential short-termer—flitting from one exotic "experience" to another. He always managed to swing light class schedules, top-of-the-line stereo equipment, and female tour guides. Joe was even planning a little business venture—shipping cameras back to the states.

I spent a lot of time preparing my Bible classes and thought I was finally getting a foothold in the deeply secular minds of my students. I worked hard to present the living God to people who had no concept of the transcendant. Joe and the others seemed content repeating the clichés they had absorbed from religious backgrounds.

What really irritated me was how little some of the student missionaries tried to adapt to their new environment. Simple things like eating with chopsticks or removing one's shoes at the doorway became for them traumatic changes. And then there was the *ofuro*.

Our Japanese-style bathtub was heated by a small gas stove which had to be carefully regulated. My roommates were always on the verge of blowing it up. I had to constantly watch lest they turn on the heater without filling up the tub, or turn on the gas without a flame, or, as seemed to happen all the time, leave the thing on for the next guy—who never came.

Tossing and turning on my damp sheet, I felt a bit guilty about my flood of criticism. I reached for more charitable thoughts but a drowsy prayer trickled away into half-conscious ramblings. If only Joe would learn how to work the *ofuro* right. Still haven't heard him come in yet. Wonder who he's out messing around with this time.

Meanwhile, back at the English school, Joe was deep in conversation with Junko. She had been asking a lot of questions in Bible classes about prayer and God's will. The girl had prayed about something very important to her and God had answered No. It was such a reasonable request. "Surely a merciful God would answer a prayer like that," she told Joe.

The student missionary began explaining the way God had guided him in his life. He shared some very personal problems and how God had dealt with them. Junko listened. These were words she had always needed to hear. No one had really *showed* her how God worked.

"For example," Joe explained further, "you know how much I like Betty, but I'm praying that God's will be done in the matter. I want to be part of His plan."

"What? Even about your girlfriend? I didn't think anybody could do that—be willing to give up such a thing to God." Junko was genuinely amazed.

"You're right. No one can do that, but with Christ it's a different story." Joe went on to tell the girl why God's will had become something he could trust. Junko was moved. And Joe had the thrill of seeing this often-perplexed student break through to a new understanding of God's activity.

After the long train ride to our house in the suburbs, Joe was ready for a good sleep. But, stepping through our doorway, he heard water gurgling and splashing somewhere inside. He opened the bathroom door and immediately lurched back as steam poured out into the hallway. Joe could hardly see or breathe, but managed to feel his way to the gas switch and turn off the *ofuro* heater. The boiling water quieted and the steam slowly cleared. Joe peered cautiously into our bathroom. The rubber mat which covered our tub had been warped into a saddle shape by the intense heat, but fortunately the tub was undamaged.

As it turned out it was me, ultracareful Mosley, who lay peacefully snoring, had left the *ofuro* on full blast from 10:30 p.m. to 1:00 a.m.

The next morning at breakfast, Joe wasn't at all upset when he told us about the near disaster. It was just another anecdote—"the night I was mugged by a raging *ofuro*." And he also told us about how Junko had opened up. Joe did get excited about that.

Junko. She was in some of my Bible classes. I had discoursed at great length in trying to answer her questions—but. . . .

Bam. Right between the eyes. Skillfully wielding chopsticks over a bowl of rice and mushroom soup, I listened to Joe and felt the Lord's telling blow. It was a rude but valuable awakening. I needed it. I had to be dethroned from my elevated easy chair of self-righteousness.

After that morning I began to see God's graciousness in Joe. I listened more carefully to what he was planning for his Bible classes, and even learned to appreciate the quality of his stereo headphones.

And the *ofuro* never rumbled again.

Love is patient.

—1 Corinthians 13:4, NASB.

Chapter 5

Adela

So many other tastes have interposed since then and confused or diluted the memory of those first foods. But I can still see Adela rolling mashed potatoes in spicy tortillas beside the deep kitchen sink. She would quarter dewy mangoes, fry long, thick banana slices, and stir the rice and beans together while I loitered by the stove, in-between mischief, all the while growing hungrier. I can still see her supple, bronze hands as they worked the cornmeal with stone mortar and pestle. At last she would bring the feast into the curtained dining room where the family smiled from dignified chairs.

From this distance, the realization of what a meek, gracious servant she was, carries a piquant edge. But for her, this humble state was invisible. Like a fish's ocean, it stretched out infinitely.

Other scenes linger vividly like something learned by heart. There was the time I thought I had been mercilessly abandoned. My parents and brothers had somehow vanished over the earth's edge, down the street, for an hour's epoch. I wept in terror on Adela's lap. She, like a great painting animated only in the essential part, sat silent against the slow evening light from the window, gazing calmly into a great distance, and stroked my head.

Yes, I suppose we always prayed for her, along with the missionaries around the world and Uncle Chet who had something gloomy called cancer. We petitioned from the eldest down to me once a week in the living room.

She had come from the mountains, where Indian folk are rooted in the soil for better or for worse and, ever barefoot, are by the very earth shod. In those green highlands, life moves in rhythm and brims with labor.

One stretch of labor had produced for Adela a private glory—her son. He stood gallantly in a photograph on the shelf that bore her possessions. How she had beamed when the picture first came of Eduardo posed with glowing diploma in front of the national university. He had graduated with honors, honors she treasured as tokens from his world.

One interminable Sunday I grew ambitious. Why not teach her to read and write. After all, somebody had taught me. She protested, of course, but my naive enthusiasm prevailed. So Adela slowly sat down after watching me spread papers and notebook on the faded roses of our kitchen tablecloth. I printed out a few letters and she obligingly coaxed the pencil into crawling uncertainly after them. I knew she could do it.

But soon, roller skates, marathon Monopoly, and fighting World War II with my buddy, Gabrielito, swallowed up the teaching career. And Adela returned to her radio and solitary meditations.

Yes, we prayed. Sometimes by God's grace the earnest, guileless prayers of children ascended. But Adela inhabits a place where only images carry weight. She has been hemmed in by candled saints and offerings that the street dogs devour in secret. For her, Christ is a wooden figure that bleeds paint, carried above a drunken crowd on holy days. How can her thoughts ascend to Him?

And then we left. My mother and Adela wept. I packed my best marbles and roller-skated in the patio for the last time. Adela went back up into the village where the aged can still recognize most of life—and I discovered America. New worlds of good and evil opened up—television, football, and frustrating females.

But the family kept in touch. Adela would send a letter every Christmas. Down in the village square where unclaimed animals and naked children mingle on the packed dirt, a white-shirted country gentleman always sat with his typewriter. To him Adela would go with her thoughts. Flourishing hands over the keys, he would transform her message into a flowery, formal proclamation of intent, so to speak. But behind his effusive grammar, Adela's ageless heart still appeared.

The outline of Adela's face faded steadily as I passed through high school and college. The countenances of the great in history and the faces of many friends captured my attention. But one link remained. The prayer. Sometimes the link thinned— one request among many. But her name persisted in my thoughts. If only she could catch a glimpse of Christ.

You wonder how though, up there in the mountains, with a clump of adobe walls and a well. No word on a page can touch her. How can the message I hear men continually try to wrestle into our privileged heads, ever reach, much less penetrate, her mind.

I kept wondering and kept praying until one day I heard. It came in the faithful Christmas letter. A couple of lines. They overtook me slowly. "I have become a Christian. In all my life I've never been so happy." The words sunk in and hit a nerve. Adela! All these years. How? ... Who? ... I could only read again and again, "Christian ... happy," and wonder, can it really be that our ragged petitions somehow aid God in striking home that priceless blow of grace thousands of miles away?

Come to think of it, there's Uncle Chet too. Once eaten up, almost gone, now he grows old slowly like everyone else, somehow.

After my hearty congratulations, Adela sent back the village typists's expressions signed in large letters by her own hand. From the convoluted language these phrases leaped out like fireworks, "... always a son to me. ... Please pray for me. ... I have many great battles ... speaking of Him to many ... if we don't meet in this life ... in Heaven."

For God . . . made his light shine in our hearts.

—2 Corinthians 4:6, NIV.

Chapter 6

Homely Glass

Jeannie stood in front of a whiteboard smudged with the felt-pen remains of level-six English drills. Her face clouded over like an ominous sky. "I'm not *doing* anything, Reiko. I just don't know how."

Reiko stared at her friend, taken aback by the sudden force of her declaration. "What do you mean, 'I'm not doing anything'?"

Jeannie looked away. "I'm a lousy Bible-class teacher, that's all there is to it."

Reiko's thoughts flashed back to other student missionaries who had come to Japan and the Himeji school where she worked as a secretary. She recalled their similar moments of truth. "Jeannie, I know how you feel right now. But you can't really expect people to respond so soon. It's only been a month since you came here. In Japan it sometimes takes students a long time to accept Christ. Like Tokiko, that friend of mine in Osaka; it took her four years to make a decision."

Instead of clearing, the "weather" around Jeannie's face clouded thickly. "That's not the problem. It's not that students aren't responding. It's me. I'm not giving them the good news, or anything worthwhile, for that matter. You know I just barely survive that one hour a week, trying to make time pass." Suddenly Jeannie's words tumbled through an unruly crowd of tears, "Oh Reiko, I'm just not good enough to teach the Bible."

Reiko thought she had the problem nailed this time. Leaning closer, she counseled, "That's exactly the same feeling I had right before I started leading a Bible-study group a few years ago. The director of the Osaka English School asked me to teach one of the Bible classes there. Well, I wasn't sure I wanted to get that involved, and I had some pretty good excuses, such as, 'I only got baptized three months ago and you want me to teach? I don't have any great experiences to share, and I know almost nothing about the Bible.' But fortunately, those excuses weren't good enough for him. He told me, 'If you wait ten years to get ready, you'll never do it. You'll end up like some church members, warming a church pew but never sharing the Lord with anybody.'"

Reiko searched Jeannie's face for some sign that light was breaking through, and continued, "The director said it didn't matter how long I had been a Christian or how much I knew about the Bible. What mattered was that I had accepted Christ. That made me good enough to witness. You know, I'm so glad I started sharing then. That became my first Christian experience. I saw God's power and wisdom work through me. That was really exciting."

Jeannie looked down at the rug, anticlimactically silent. Reiko kept trying. "Jeannie, most Japanese don't know anything about Jesus. Some of them have never heard the name. But you know Him, and that's what makes you good enough to teach others."

When Jeannie finally glanced up, she spoke out of a well of helplessness. "You don't understand. I should never have come as a student missionary." The American girl gathered up the tattered remains of her missionary dream and blurted out, "I don't know Christ. That's why I can't get anything across."

Reiko, so eager before to assure, now balked before this confession. Only one thought managed to break loose in her mind—somehow, Jeannie's being there must be God's will. Reiko had prayed so hard that the Lord would send the right people to her school. When the three teachers came in June, she had had no doubts. Whatever problems they might pass through, she was sure God had great blessings in store.

And so, in the low, graying light that remained after the heat of an August afternoon, Jeannie and Reiko spread out their problem before the Lord. As they rose from their knees, Reiko pictured what Jeannie must have been going through the past few weeks—those questions: "Why do you believe in God?" and "How do you know He's really there?"—hitting with unexpected force, exposing a whole array of unexamined beliefs one never had to explain in a Christian environment. The secretary caught a ray of light. "Hey Jeannie, why don't we study the Word and prepare for our Bible classes together? We'll get to know God better and maybe receive new insights we can use in our teaching."

So the two girls from the edges of the biggest ocean began. They chose a few New Testament parables and, instead of just getting a general spiritual lesson out of the stories, wrote down as many practical principles as they could find in each parable. They tried to apply these principles in their daily life and challenged their Bible students to use them.

Almost immediately Jeannie and her Bible classes began to perk up. God had broken her down to that one essential starting point—knowing Him. The well of helplessness spawned a new perspective. Students began to notice a different spirit in her. One lady asked whether she could have private Bible lessons. Several other acquaintances made the same request, and soon Jeannie was happily "sacrificing" more and more of her time sharing the good news individually.

A few months later as Jeannie was elaborating on the joys of being a Christian, she noticed a puzzled look on a familiar face in the room. After class she walked over to his desk. "What's bothering you, Hiro?"

Hiro looked up, hesitating for a second. "I just don't see any reason why I need Christ. I think I'm happy and satisfied. I don't really need much more of anything."

All the edifying words that were supposed to gush forth on such occasions got lost somewhere in the recesses of Jeannie's mind. She started firing up inaudible rounds of "Lord, give me *something*." Even if she could have launched into a profound explanation, Hiro would have only understood half of her English.

Suddenly, Jeannie turned and picked up a blue felt pen. On the whiteboard she outlined a picture of an empty glass. "Let's suppose this is your heart, OK? Now tell me how full the glass is." Hiro stood up and drew a line on the board. "I see your glass is about 85 percent full. Wouldn't you like it to be full clear to the top?" she asked expectantly.

Hiro pondered the drawing for a heavy moment. "You know, I don't see any big difference between 100 percent full and 85 percent. Fifteen percent more is not going to give me that much more satisfaction. I'm happy enough now."

Jeannie felt suddenly weightless. She knew Hiro was well-liked and usually cheerful. How could she express to him his need for Christ? Then again the friction between a prayer-oriented mind and the divine eagerness produced a spark. Jeannie sketched water pouring down into the glass and overflowing. "What if Christ not only fills up your glass but also gives overflowing happiness and joy?" The spark touched something faintly flammable in Hiro's introspection. Jeannie continued. "Where does this overflowing water go? Is it going to be wasted?" As Hiro's eyes widened slightly, Jeannie answered her own question. "It flows out to other people. Christ not only makes you happy but also makes everybody around you happy. Don't you want to bring happiness to all your friends?"

That did it. For reasons only the Spirit knows, that homely glass scrawled on the whiteboard, penetrated where an erudite speech would have been ineffective. That picture unlocked the mystery. Through one now firmly connected, Christ's love ignited into authentic flame. Hiro's voice transparently eager, was almost laughter. "Yes! I want Jesus. I want Jesus! Please teach me about Jesus!"

Your mercy, O Lord, is in the heavens.

—Psalm 36:5, NKJV.

Chapter 7

... Something to Happen

By the time we straggled back on the bus after eight hours in the furniture factory, our limbs were pretty well gone. They had passed through the same motions, attentive to the one duty endlessly repeated, until muscle was one long groan.

It was a strange kind of exhaustion. Very different from the mellow tiredness following a long football game. It left us drained and numb. We didn't talk much on the bus heading back to the dorm. We were all thinking of something to happen.

We rode a dusty gravel road past the flat stretches of Illinois cornfields. Nothing but miles and miles of corn around. Nothing but a dull flat sky above us.

Our dorm was almost empty. The one across the campus was totally desolate. Only a few unrich, unconnected guys got stuck at the school's furniture shop all summer. There were five of us to be exact—five homely souls in limbo.

Jack, the packer, was a lanky, shy, hard worker. He sometimes told me tall tales about some isolated mountain school, where women were not allowed to expose their limbs and Monopoly was considered decadent. Jack seemed to be laboring against a divine law that stretched from horizon to horizon. There was no escape from its endless requirements. He never complained and rarely laughed.

Tod was my freshman roommate. I, a Senior, believed that a vast gulf separated us and that the lad was not yet fully conscious. He talked about cars too much.

Alf, who stapled drawers, appeared a bit older and had been through some pretty rough times in the world. He was sure that a little dark cloud followed him around everywhere. Once after supper we were walking across campus and he pointed up and, sure enough, a little dark cloud was following him around. Alf suspected that God played favorites.

Alf's brother Rod was too amiable to question the Almighty. But then, like most of the rest of us, he wasn't curious either. Sure, we'd heard about God beaming down in love since cradle roll, but the guys felt something a bit more ominous overhead. They shared an unspoken commitment to leave the wide, gray sky alone as much as possible.

It wasn't a bad summer really. It was just that nothing big ever happened. At the factory we had to work pretty hard to come up with something truly distracting. Like staple fights, for instance. Elaborate cardboard defenses had to be erected— secret alliances worked out.

The guys who put sides on dressers had the obvious advantage. Their staple guns could sting at fifteen yards. The climax of the sport came unexpectedly one day when Alf shot at a pesky fly, stapling the unfortunate creature right across the neck to a deacon bench. The fly lay there as if carefully mounted for exhibition.

Often the highlight of our day was the thirty minutes following the noon buzzer when we could climb up on stacks of flat cardboard toward the cool ceiling and eat potato chips and tomato sandwiches. We luxuriated in being as immobile as possible.

We were counting the hours, the minutes, the trips to the bathroom. The students tried hard to get on "piece-time" so they could have something to hurry about, some way to escape the empty horizon-to-horizon hours. But most paid-by-the-piece jobs were reserved for the older men. With nothing to work for, we just put in time, doing what was required.

We were always looking for something to happen—looking for a legitimate event.

On Sabbaths we were driven to the town of La Fox. It provided one store, three houses, and an address for the academy. In an upstairs room a few saints gathered to accompany a tiny, whiny organ.

Each Sabbath Jack faithfully carried a miniature pack of poker cards in his inside suit coat pocket. If a sermon got a bit too pressing he could always reach in and finger the ace of spades or queen of hearts. The poker cards were his security, preventing the angels from getting too close.

I admitted that church was an earnest attempt at an event. But I didn't always get the message. Often I would remember the few "religious" types I had seen around school. They were a peculiar breed—always wore white shirts, looked nervous and spoke in King James English. I had not known anyone who took them seriously.

Some weekdays we did manage to create modest entertainments. One night, for instance, the guys on second floor were doing card tricks. Suddenly, Alf told me to stand very still and concentrate on his hands. He pointed his two index fingers at my eyes and came closer and closer. Alf touched my closed eyelids and at the same instant something touched my shoulder. No one else was around.

For a split second it was incomprehensible. Somebody really did touch my shoulder! I was pierced by wonder. A miracle! The supernatural had come into our flat, drab little world. But the second of awe passed as I realized Alf had touched my eyes with the forked fingers of only one hand and struck me with the other.

We were looking for something to happen. Each day was the same bus ride to the factory, the same dull motions for eight hours and the same trip home to slouch around into the night and listen wistfully to Stevie Wonder's, "My Cherie Amour."

One Sunday the old school bus took us to a park nearby. We went swimming and spotted two girls frolicking in the shallow end of the pool. Once in a while they would peek our way, shyly, and giggle. I'm sure they were no great beauties, scarcely more than skinny, toothy adolescents. But to our deprived senses, they seemed like goddesses from that distance. Their every movement inspired admiration.

Alf made great noises about what he was going to do—in a minute. Jack stared, very low in the water. Tod tried to get their attention by talking loudly. Rod laughed amiably, and I splashed around a lot.

In the end, we dried off and slunk back into the bus without ever speaking a word to the two achingly beautiful aliens. Nothing happened.

Actually, that summer we did witness one historic event. The dean actually brought out an ancient twelve-inch, black-and-white TV for us to watch the astronauts land on the moon. We started watching at midnight. Since the astronauts took their time about it, half of us could hardly stay awake. Armstrong did finally descend the Eagle's ladder, but I had only one eye open at the time.

We witnessed something great, but through a long, dark tunnel. The event didn't touch us.

OK, I admit the dean brought the TV out a few other times. One night we had a variety show. A comedian made a rat do tricks—on an elephant's stool. The man had a huge whip. . . . I rolled on the floor with laughter. This was the funniest thing ever recorded by man. All the bleak hours in the factory poured out of me in uncontrolled merriment. Quite therapeutic, but it was all over so soon, almost before it happened.

On another day we decided to outsmart the "factory blues." We were sick and tired of walking around like zombies, wasted from monotonous labor. We decided to play football in the evening and get some legitimate exhaustion.

So we threw ourselves into it, running and tackling hard till we couldn't stand up. We felt our lungs ache. This was good. This was how the body should feel—wonderfully worn out, used up.

But I couldn't get the guys to play after that. Alf nursed his right knee. Jack wanted to listen to the radio. We slid back into physical limbo.

Still, we wanted something to happen. But nothing really did—until a few weeks before school started when Clint came. He hailed from the West Coast. California seemed a rather exotic place. Things happened there.

The first thing that struck us about Clint was that he worked rather cheerfully. He was stuck in the paint room at the end of the assembly line, a noxious place, which left you with a slight sense of intoxication by the end of the day. Clint painted dressers and cabinets smiling as if he were not all there. Oh, he was alert all right, but somehow he wasn't all there in that gloomy factory.

He'd been places, not just geographical ones. His life was going somewhere. He had goals for the future. How could anybody have goals surrounded by miles of nothing but corn?

Clint was sincere, never pretentious, and never corny. We noticed him say grace at meals, but he never wore a white shirt. That was a new trick.

Something somehow made him terribly content. We couldn't figure it out. Once in a while he even talked about things he had read in the Bible, but he didn't speak King James English.

It didn't actually all hit me till one Friday evening. Walking back from supper, I noticed traces of purple, orange, and magenta in the sky. Quite a sunset. I had not noticed too many sunsets before. Toward the west the sun was flaring out and its golden rays were reflected in scattered clouds all the way across the heavens. I had never seen so much color. The flat gray ceiling was alive with color. And then I noticed Clint sitting alone out on the football field bleachers.

Clint was out there with his Bible, looking at the sunset too. It was then that it struck me—the place was friendly, I mean the big place, the Universe. At least Clint was comfortable with it. He was getting ready for the Sabbath, in his own way.

Nobody had told him what to do. There were no rules proscribing bleacher-sitting on the Lord's day. Clint was making something happen. He wasn't just putting in time.

I looked out over the expanse of rolling hills turning purple in the haze. Maybe the Almighty *was* beaming down. Maybe there was a rest from the endless limbo. Maybe religion could be part of your own life.

There above the cornfields, God seemed to have an affable voice. It was something Clint could hear.

The sun, digging deeper into the horizon, cut a majestic path far ahead through the clouds. Very inviting.

After staring a long, long time, I made my way slowly toward the bleachers.

He was led as a lamb to the slaughter.

—Isaiah 53:7, NIV.

Chapter 8

Hey Duck!

The trouble was, we could never quite figure Harold out. He just didn't fit into any recognizable mold at our academy. To some of the guys he seemed aloof.

For example, although he might be present, Harold never really was a part of our daily evening ritual. In between supper and "study hall" the guys would sprawl around our porch, gaze idly across campus to the girls' dorm, and pass around comments about the sad state of affairs over there. Harold always sat on the end of a bench, his plump hands wandering over his knees, and laughed temperately at our jokes with both eagerness and distance. Under short, wheat-colored hair, his clear eyes stared elsewhere.

Harold didn't work like the rest of us on the grounds crew either. We were veterans at wasting time by the hour, slow motion experts who knew how to spend time hoeing a weed, teasing it to death leaf by leaf. Smooth shifts into high gear were reserved for when the boss rounded a corner. We expended most of our energies swapping stories or scheming for a ride on the dump truck.

Harold never could get into the spirit of the thing. He always managed to remain occupied at some useful task even when there were legitimate reasons for standing around. Harold didn't make a big deal out of his conscientious work habits. When we kidded him, he only replied that he liked to put in "real time."

And Harold seemed to be one of the few who were fazed by our campus worships. At chapel, most of the guys were careful to slouch and look coolly disinterested. We were all but immunized to the Gospel from our chronic indifference to small doses of it over the years. It was considered a mark of manhood to have passed through many altar calls "unscathed"—unsurrendered.

But Harold always listened reverently during worship talks. Somehow, that realm of angels and "Thou Shalt Nots" meant something to him. And yet the kid didn't have the self-conscious oddity we expected in religious types. He seemed comfortable with Jesus and his Bible.

The guys were baffled by this creature. To top it off, Harold was hopeless with girls, too awkward for football, and besides, he liked Bach—whatever that was.

Though different, Harold was quiet, and not many could quarrel with his simple courtesy. He wanted to belong, and maintained his amiable quietness until one evening circumstances forced his hand.

The dean was gone and Jack, president of the Boys Club, had to give worship. As we assembled in the lobby, Jack sat on the monitor's desk and thumbed through one of those "Daily Fragrance" books. He felt uneasy in his role as "preacher" and began a desultory reading of one short passage. "The Christian life is a struggle on the upward path. Only through divine power may success be attained." Occasionally Jack glanced up and smirked at his captive audience.

The boys began to laugh, tentatively at first, then with enthusiasm. "We can bear any trial with this love and peace abiding in our hearts," Jack intoned. "Amens" echoed through the lobby. "Lay it on me brother Jack."

Encouraged, Jack read on, mimicking a pulpiteer's drone. "Let us march on the narrow path and not relinquish our call until we reach Heaven's Gate."

"Oh Glory! Heaven's Gate!" We shouted, caught up in our ersatz revival. This was fun.

Jack's devotional reading concluded with a chorus of "hallelujahs." He was inspired to pray sarcastically. We had never been irreverent during prayer before. A direct address to God had always drawn a measure of deference even from our calloused souls. But the momentum of our escape from years of enforced, passive listening to worship talks, carried us through the last barrier.

Jack began grandiosely, "Lord of highest heaven . . ." and then, perhaps catching himself, continued more simply, "thanks for all these great words and everything. We had a wonderful worship." A jumble of saintly exclamations drowned the "Amen."

Suddenly a voice cut through our gaiety. It was Harold, speaking subversive words. He stood trembling between fear and anger. "You guys are the most sacrilegious bunch I've ever seen." The kid stared at our surprised faces for a moment and then turned abruptly toward his room.

Someone recovered his senses and shouted down the hall, "Who do ya think *you* are Harold?" As we dispersed from our makeshift sanctuary everyone joined in deprecating "that self-righteous squirrel."

For the next few days the incident seemed forgotten. But Harold's fate was sealed. He had bucked the "system" and his challenge could not be ignored. And so, in a hushed gathering late one night, "The Duck," was born.

Watching Harold from behind as he moved his pudgy thighs in his baggy pants, someone had detected a hint of a waddle in his gait. The Duck! A perfect nickname! Finally we had an identity for the "alien" in our midst.

On the sidewalks in between classes, the guys began to call out, "Hey, Duck," and laugh at his embarrassment. The words were always hurled from a distance, like a projectile. For weeks Harold endured in grim silence.

But one day in the cafeteria he broke. Harold had just scraped his tray clean and was walking out when Mack, the campus clown, called out, "Hey Duck, what's happening?" Harold kept walking. Others joined in, "Duck, Duck, hey Duck." At the glass doors Harold stopped and swung around. His features were compressed, as if passing through a barrier.

He lifted both hands in an obscene gesture and shook them at the guys, livid with a helpless rage.

Everyone roared. The "alien" had spoken our language and, for a moment, taken on our likeness.

Late that evening, in the restless lull before "lights-out," the guys started wondering where "The Duck" was. Lowly freshmen, given new status by this outcast, wondered the loudest, "He must be up to something." Someone knocked on Harold's door. "Hey Duck, what are you doing in there?" No sound.

Several guys pounded on the door, "Hey Duck, come out a minute." Other doors opened and the hallway filled with those eager for some excitement. A score of fists began hammering on the flimsy door and cinder-block walls of Harold's small hiding place.

Some began shouting angrily. They couldn't get a squeak out of room 109. Then a voice broke out, loud and long, "Quack, Quack, Quaaaack." Instantly all joined in, "Quack, Qua, Qua, Quaaack," creating a mass of sound that rocked the hall.

The duck call reverberated through the dormitory for five minutes . . . ten minutes. . . . In the dim hallway, flailing arms were silhouetted eerily against the yellow exit light. Voices so recently raised in "hallelujahs," now hurled their epithet at the unseen adversary like those casting a spell. The chant pounded harder and harder against the walls, building hypnotically into a jagged rumble.

Suddenly the lights came on. The guys turned with the wild sound half-way up their throats. Dean Ross stood by the fire escape, leaning against a wall with his pen and demerit cards. He spoke wearily, "OK boys, knock it off. Everybody in your room. C'mon, let's go." Ross turned off the lights and waited as the guys scattered, some with lingering smiles.

But after the dean left and everything quieted, no one joked. "The Duck" was still silent in his room. An uncanny presence seemed to hover in the vacant hall. A few of the guys peered from their rooms with solemn faces. The silence was oppressively heavy. The hallway stared back at us, gaunt, almost tomblike.

It has been many years since "The Duck" attended our academy. I wish I knew what became of him. Harold stayed out the year, still courteous, but armed with a new, hard-edged reticence. After spring quarter finals, I never saw him again.

There are things I wish I could say to Harold now. The pain inflicted on him still haunts me. I can't forget the look of the hunted animal in his face, or our hard, piercing voices in the night.

Now, too late, I see a unique, gracious human being in the one we dismissed as an ugly duck. In his gentle uprightness Harold was something of a swan. And I still wonder why we could not bear that quiet beauty during his short stay among us.

How can I give you up, Ephraim?

Chapter 9

Homesick

Our summer camp was lusciously green. Set around a shimmering, cool lake, it harbored a plethora of adolescent pleasures: canoe rides, water-skiing, horseback riding, crafts, and campfires. A fresh new world of cattails, hickory, and frogs by the water's edge invited exploration. In between scheduled activities, there was always a pillow fight or a game of kick-the-can to keep things hopping.

But one seven-year-old in my cabin wasn't completely happy in this paradise. Something kept gnawing at Billy, especially as he lay on his bunk after "lights out." Finally, the red-haired, freckle-faced boy unburdened himself to me, "I think I've learned enough now. I think they need me at home."

"Billy don't you think your folks can manage without you for a week?" I asked.

Billy continued, "And the food here is kind of funny."

"You don't like the food?"

"Well . . . I may get sick."

"You look pretty healthy to me."

"But I don't feel so good."

"That's too bad—out here in all this fresh air, with the trees and squirrels and . . ."

"And yesterday I cut my finger. Remember? See?"

"Just a scratch Billy."

"You know it could be real dangerous out here. . . ." The boy paused and looked out a window. "I think my mother needs me."

Failing to convince Billy of the wonderful time he was having at camp, I informed the camp director that I had one for the road. Mr. Logan, however, was anxious that his campers stick it out for the duration. He believed that homesickness is an emotional barrier that, once hurdled, proves much less formidable the next time around. So the director invited Billy into his office for a little chat.

Billy was very quiet and polite, but not even the camp director's try-it-one-more-day offer could release the boy's white-knuckled grasp on the hope of going home *now*. Mr. Logan called the camper's mother.

Back in the cabin, Billy packed his old, gray suitcase with immense relief and waited, staring at the bare pine ceiling.

After the boy had asked me what time it was for the eleventh time, we got word that his mother was down in the parking lot. I carried the heavy suitcase and Billy skipped along ahead of me. Having seen the light come on in the kid's eyes, I was expecting some warm, loving woman to jump out of a car and run up to embrace her youngster. But as we broke the tree-lined path and walked up to a dusty Packard, we were met by a sloppily-dressed, glum-faced matron strolling back to open up the trunk of the car. She gave her son a casual, graceless greeting. I waited in vain for some little show of affection to break through the woman's tepid exterior.

But Billy didn't seem to mind—he had been found. In the twinkling of an eye he had come out of a dark, alien land to the promise of home sweet home. The first sighting of his mother had done it; he rested content in her ungainly presence.

The woman bid me a gruff Good day and drove off. Billy was too preoccupied with his rescue to wave back at me through the rear window.

I haven't been able to forget that boy's blissful face in the droopy Packard or the way he placed all his security and happiness in the lap of that mother who seemed so utterly unattractive. The bare, filial tie that riveted him to her side seemed to have the out-of-proportion power of an atomic bond.

Billy's being so lost and so found gave me, quite unexpectedly, a glimpse of Christ and His intense love. I usually pictured Jesus as our elder brother or father. But that day He seemed, in a sense, very much like Billy, the devoted son.

Christ's longing for the citizens of this indifferent planet is elemental and inexplicable. There is little in us to attract His devotion. Our love is fickle and shallow. It doesn't even nudge the scale when compared with Christ's self-sacrificing regard.

Yet Jesus always behaves as if His security is tied up with ours. He is restless when we wander and agonizes over our separation from Him. He pleads for reunion. Christ did not consider heaven a place to be cherished while we were lost.

For a moment, freckle-faced Billy filled me with wonder. I saw the self-existent One painfully homesick for the unlovely and unlovable ones who cut themselves off from Him. I realized His is a homesickness that nothing can turn aside.

There is no greater love than this, that a man should lay down his life for his friends.

—John 15:13, NEB.

Chapter 10

The Cutting Edge

At 7:05 P.M. ambulance No. 2 sped from McDonough County Hospital with red lights flashing and roared down Highway 136 toward the town of Bushnell. The dispatch on the dashboard was brief: "Car wreck."

Sitting in the back beside the stretcher, I watched trees whiz by and wondered how this call would turn out. You never could tell. Most of the frantic people phoning the hospital in an emergency tended to exaggerate.

There was that call from Colchester—the lady whose husband was "having a heart attack." We rushed over to the town, sirens wailing and lights flashing, made a wrong turn right in the middle of Colchester with all the folks who had emptied Ralph's Drugstore and Jane's Cafe staring at us, backed up, roared off again, and finally ferreted out 1345 Lockwood. The three of us, loaded with resucitation equipment, ran up to the door and asked the lady as we brushed past, "Where is he?"

"Oh," she replied politely, "he's in the bedroom getting dressed."

Even the recent collision between a pickup and a locomotive (which I was sure would be a sight) had resulted only in a few minor scratches. It seemed it was always the eleven-to-seven guys who got the really bad stuff.

Darkness settled over the broad Illinois cornfields as we raced toward the accident. Rounding a curve just south of Bushnell we came upon a crowd of people and two police cars beside the

55

road. One decrepit pickup leaned into a drainage ditch. Another false alarm, I thought.

But then I saw it—out in the field. A Chevy that had once been white. It was crumpled up about thirty yards out in the freshly plowed field. The car had turned end-over-end several times to get there from the highway.

The Chevy lay there alone, speckled in the moonlight. Spectators lining the road maintained their distance. Even the police did not go near. Sure sign of a mess.

A sheriff walked up and asked Dave, our driver, to radio a report to the county coroner. I was relieved. At least there would be no screaming.

Clutching my attendant's bag, I walked slowly over the deep furrows with the other orderly. We peered reluctantly through a smashed window. Our flashlight picked out legs sprawled on the seat, one shoe missing; head and chest lay on the floorboard. But he was all in one piece.

Then our beam of light hit the man's face. His eyes stared back from the floorboard, wide open and full of terror.

I had seen other deaths before in the hospital. Those in the geriatric ward who slipped away by inches simply closed their eyes in a deeper sleep. And I had seen violent deaths—people in the early morning fog whose life had suddenly been wrenched away by a windshield. But their eyes seemed benumbed, reflecting only quiet surprise.

This poor man however, though dead, still shouted. His gaze pierced. In his face one could read the sudden swerve off the road, the grip torn from the steering wheel, and the wild tumbling before the final blow to his head. Terror, fully tasted, shone from his grey eyes—"Help!" But we maintained our "professional calm."

We straightened his limbs respectfully and managed to maneuver him out of the car and onto our stretcher. Dave tied the white mortuary gown around his still form. We struggled with his unwieldy bulk across the furrows to our ambulance.

The wind kept whipping at the "body bag." I prayed that he would stay covered. My bare arms felt an unusual chill. Autumn apparently had come in earnest.

I had lifted other bodies from mangled cars. In the rush of well-rehearsed duties, the human element was usually hidden. Sometimes the dead were strangely unreal, like dolls we lifted, covered, and put gently away.

But this dark night everything was different. The man's piercing gaze had disarmed my "emergency medical technician" pretenses.

On our return, as I rode in the back alone with the body, I was just a scared kid. The man's feet swayed with the motions of the ambulance. I couldn't get my mind off his eternally terrified expression under the linen.

That night I had my first encounter with death in the raw. Before it had always had its cosmetic covering. Like the funeral that same year at our church. An elderly lady, bent and withered from decades of hard labor, had passed away. In an elegant coffin in our church foyer, she looked almost better than in "real life." The mortician had added color to her cheeks, straightened her limbs a bit, and simulated a properly peaceful countenance.

At the cemetery, lofty eulogies and shiny brass belied the presence of a corpse. No indiscrete dirt was visible. Plastic grass covered the mound, and a welter of bouquets the grave. We commemorated the abstract idea of this lady's passing.

But in that smashed Chevy, I came face to face with the real thing—death's cutting edge, wrenching loss. We rarely go gently into the night. Frequently, life is ripped from our hands.

Perhaps we Christians have flowered and ornamented Christ's death into a mere abstraction. We give assent to the idea of His passing, but we do not see its visceral drama. The cross—it's such a familiar theological category. We celebrate it in the comfortable and dignified confines of a sanctuary. It's hard to really touch the wrenching violence of that event.

But in that accident victim's eyes I believe I caught a glimpse of the death of Christ. Our Saviour did not go gently into the night either. He was tossed about in the violent currents between heaven and earth, tortured by man, seemingly abandoned by God.

Jesus gave Himself up to the ordeal of crucifixion with His eyes wide open. He knew full well the dimensions of the sacrifice required of Him. It wasn't easy. Christ clung to the cold earth of Gethsemane and sought in vain the comfort of human companions before facing the Jewish "welcoming committee" armed with swords and clubs.

His naked body writhing on the cross was no "death in disguise." It was a spectacle, designed to pierce our hearts and minds. No colleagues eulogized Christ's "untimely passing." No flowers covered the hole in the earth. He endured a naked act of violence. The self-destructiveness of our sin tore Him apart.

And yet, somehow in the midst of His wild tumbling between heaven and earth, Jesus bound a disciple to His heart-broken mother, and offered salvation to a repentant thief.

Christ refused the anesthetizing wine and gall. He was fully aware until the last. He saw the vicious mocking of those He had come to save. And all of sin, the whole compounded horror—from Assyria's skinned captives to the human pyramids at Auschwitz—beat at His soul. Christ gazed at the whole ghastly train of human cruelty and accepted its guilt.

He was all alone on that barren stretch of Golgotha. No one would come near. With religious officials aloof, friends at a distance, and soldiers gambling for His garments, Jesus hung isolated in a night vast and unmarked.

I think that is the ultimate measure of His courage. He faced hell open-eyed. He faced the brunt of what no man can bear. Christ looked at the specter of eternal separation from the Father and yet willed Himself to stay on the cross. There was no cushioning for His coffin. He absorbed the shock of an evil that causes nature herself to groan. By the blows He suffered, we are healed.

He is our servant, carried off and wrapped in linen. And we, His privileged attendants, walk beside, dressed in the white garments of His righteousness.

Then what can separate us from the love of Christ? Can affliction or hardship? Can persecution, hunger, nakedness, peril or sword?
—Romans 8:35, NEB.

Chapter 11
Up Against the Brass

As rows of subdued waves stroked the Guam shoreline, a crescent of palms nodded off to sleep in the breeze. Two men squatting on a gnarled piece of driftwood gazed out at dusk settling over the bay.

Captain Graff's voice was calm now, even kind: "Mosley, we've got a big job to do over here; it's going to take all we've got."

"Yes sir." Chief Yeoman Ramon Mosley was even quieter.

"We're not out on some Sunday School picnic. This is war. The Navy has got to maintain complete discipline."

"Yes sir."

"Mosley," the captain sounded like a longsuffering parent. "You know what I'm going to have to do don't you?"

The chief yeoman looked down at the moist sand and replied, "Yes cap'n. What you've got to do, I guess you've just got to do."

Captain Graff slowly stood up, spit into the sea, and ambled back to the line of forest-green tents.

Mosley knew very well what his commanding officer had to do. That unnerving fact had been pressed down on him for quite some time. Anyone refusing duty in battle conditions was subject to execution. It was hard for Mosley to imagine getting shot by his own countrymen, and yet slowly, persistently, the formal confrontations were leading to that point.

The monochrome monotony of the sea stretched out before him like an unintelligible scroll. Somewhere across it's endless expanse, Frances wrote letters. For him there would be only piquant fragments. As a sailor under arrest, confined to the base, even his incoming mail was censored.

That other world where people loved, raised corn, and had reasons for life, was becoming more and more intangible. He drifted as an odd speck in a world turned upside down.

Maybe they were right. Maybe he *was* crazy. Maybe he *was* the only one holding to such bizarre convictions.

And yet, how could he forget those crystalline moments when the *truth* imposed itself on them as a compelling presence—he and Francis praying earnestly on their apartment building rooftop. Looking out over New Orleans, they had wondered out loud to their Lord about these strange new doctrines: the Sabbath—a memorial to creation and re-creation, the second coming—an imminent hope. And the Lord had answered, reviving their hearts and minds, showing them a beautiful coherence in scripture, from Eden to Eden.

For a few months, the newly-baptized newlyweds cherished an island of meaning and peace in a world convulsing madly with total war.

The test had not come at first, not until their convictions had solidified and the couple had slipped in too deep to get out. For a while, out on shore patrol in the gulf with the Navy, Mosley had been able to arrange for Saturdays off. But finally, the immovable object dropped in front of him: a direct order to work on his Sabbath.

Mosley painfully remembered the letters to Washington asking for hospital duty, refusals, changes of status, verbal blasts from an assortment of officers. It all led to one ingenious solution: "Well Mosley, we're going to see what you do on your Sabbath when the Japs get after you."

The incorrigible sailor was put on a transfer to the Solomon Islands and assigned to a Higgins landing craft unit. Surely one good landing amid machine-gun fire would cure him of his scruples.

Mosley sailed out of New Orleans on a huge transport ship. Leaning over the steel deck rail into the salty, raw gusts of the night, he knew exactly why he was being shipped out. His faith would permit no compromises. But there was no warm feeling welling up inside, no cymbals crashing. He felt only the cold wedge of conscience with which he had tried to fend off their attacks: "If you operate on what you are convinced is right, you just can't take any other stand."

Funny, it had only been four or five months since then and yet it was hard for Mosley to remember when he hadn't been surrounded by this grim, leaden ocean—always somewhere lost in it—hearing the pounding of guns, circling nameless islands, locked in meanderings comprehensible only to an elite, huddled few somewhere else.

Mosley had made chief yeoman on board ship and, as chief petty officer, was placed in charge of the personnel office on Guam after the marines established a beachhead.

For a while, he had managed to quietly arrange for time off during his Sabbath. But one Saturday the commanding officer walked into his tent and found him studying his Sabbath School lesson. The trouble began all over again.

Now as the sky blackened overhead, Mosley knew he would be facing increasing pressures to give in. But he also knew that his convictions were still in place. Mosley stood up, spit into the sea and strolled back to his quarters.

The next day a summons came from Captain Graff's tent. Mosley walked in and saluted. He knew what was coming—another "session." Graff, several executive officers, marshals, and the chaplain sat in full-dress uniform in a row around him. Their clustered brass gaudily displayed the authority which Mosley had been drilled to obey without question.

"You have a duty to your country."

"Men are being killed all around you."

"How come you're so sure you're the only one who's right?"

Each one in turn whipped out a biting monologue, threatening, pleading, shaming this man they could not fathom.

After an hour the chief yeoman's face began betraying his weariness and confusion. He couldn't answer all their accusations. Then Captain Graff struck a final swift blow: "Mosley, in this situation you have no choice. You cannot disobey a direct order. You will work on Saturday as scheduled."

Out of his haze the lone sailor managed to reply, "Sir, I have to do the only thing left for me to do. It is impossible for me to carry out . . ." He did not finish.

Graff blew up. "You WILL work Mosley." Medals and insignia shook on the captain's chest. "If you think you can defy this whole command you're in for a big surprise, sailor." Graff continued with an assortment of ear-burning epithets before thundering, "DISMISSED!"

When "deck court" finally arrived, it was almost a relief. At least the sessions would end. Mosley had at first been docketed for a court-martial. But an Adventist physician, a full commander on a Navy ship, wrote a letter to Admiral Nimitz on his behalf. He pointed out that the right of people to worship as their conscience dictated was one of the things the Navy was defending in the Pacific. Probably as a result of that letter, Mosley faced a less punitive deck court.

Beside two flags and three stiff marshals, Captain Graff read the charges and his prepared verdict. Mosley was reduced to first-class yeoman, reprimanded for insubordination, and stripped of his duties in the personnel office.

The captain then ordered him out to a rusting, decrepit barge that accommodated a few cubby-hole offices. Confined to the base, Mosley spent months in uneasy limbo, trying hard to find work that would keep him from further confrontations. But he felt grateful to have survived and for not having betrayed his Lord.

One day an ambulance pulled up near the old barges. A young man with lieutenant bars stepped out and began asking for a guy named Mosley. Everybody knew about Mosley. The yeoman was quickly brought out. He saluted and identified himself.

The lieutenant extended his hand. "Glad to meet you. I'm a Seventh-day Adventist too."

Mosley stood there for a moment stunned. He felt like a man long wandering in the desert who catches the scent of water. So there *was* another one in the world, right here in front of him. So he *wasn't* all crazy. Suddenly, tears burned in Mosley's eyes. He struggled for something to say to keep the mirage from disappearing. "How did you find out . . . I mean . . ."

"Well, our hospital ship landed on the other side last week, and I heard about this odd guy who was having trouble over his religion."

"I haven't been able to locate any Adventists since I left the States."

"Hey, well listen, there are some more SDA guys on the ship too. And we're thinking of trying to start some sort of church service here."

"Sounds great."

"I think we've got some of the Guamanians interested too. We really think this is a providential opportunity. This may be our only chance to start a church on the island."

After they retired to Mosley's tiny office, the lieutenant explained that Guam had been dominated by a powerful bishop who would permit no other religious mission to enter the island. When the Japanese took Guam they captured the bishop and sent him to the Philippines. So if the group moved fast they might be able to get something going.

"There's only one problem," the lieutenant said, "we need a place to meet."

It would always remain a complete mystery to Mosley how he managed to walk into the office of the commanding officer he had last seen at deck court. But there he was with his request, saluting a stone-faced captain Graff. "Captain," he began, "we have some Seventh-day Adventist sailors in a hospital company here who'd like to meet together, and we need some kind of place to worship in."

The commanding officer looked down at his desk and began writing. Mosley decided to go on. "I saw this old storage tent, sir, down by D barracks that nobody is using. I wonder if we could perhaps borrow it, Cap'n."

Suddenly Graff stood up and stared into the yeoman's eyes. "Listen, Mosley," he said, pointing his finger, "you don't have to use that thing. Let me get you a good tent."

The captain marched out of his office and led his awed subordinate over to a corrugated tin warehouse. There he ordered the supply officer to get Mosley a good tent, "just the size he wants."

Next Graff took Mosley over to the Lutheran chaplain. "This

man is going to start a worship service. Fix him up with whatever he needs," Graff commanded.

Quickly Mosley's arms were filled with gold and silver bowls, cups and crucifixes. Being in no position to refuse such a weighty gesture, he thanked the chaplain and left.

Graff wasn't finished. "Now, Mosley, let's see, you're going to need something to transport this stuff. Let me arrange for a truck and driver."

A truck was requisitioned and loaded. Mosley hurried off to check out at his barge. When he returned, the captain had added to the church paraphernalia a portable organ for good measure. He also had ready an unrestricted base leave for his sailor. Mosley tried to thank him, but Graff just waved him off to the truck.

Rumbling along in the truck past mangled greenery and gashes in the earth, Yeoman Mosley, first-class, carried the embryonic elements of the first Seventh-day Adventist church on Guam. He noticed a warm feeling welling up inside. He heard cymbals crashing. Mosley looked down affectionately at his unwieldy load of "holy ware." They were, in any case, symbols of a world reclaimed, vessels for celebrating that Body which had become invisible for such a long, harrowing time.

In the future, that tent would grow into a fruitful medical, educational, and evangelistic mission. But for now Ramon Mosley, my father, was brim-full just holding the seeds on the winding dusty road.

Wonderful Counselor.

—Isaiah 9:6, NIV.

Chapter 12
Detective of Doubt

My roommate, Henry, sat there furrowing his forehead over an organic chemistry textbook. It was the slow end of "study hall." Scenery had long since gone from our darkened window. Jovial, distracting voices had faded from the hallway. Soon we would hear the bell for "lights out."

My literature essay was finally out of the way. I stared at the texts spread on my bookshelf—a long row of boring titles. There was nothing to occupy my thoughts—except *the problem.*

I began pacing back and forth behind my desk, trying to work it out of my system. "Give me five good reasons why you believe in God." It was the same old line come to haunt me again. I looked outside at the street lights and started going over the answers for the hundredth time. But they all got tangled up in a fidgety, internal dialogue.

How can you be so sure that the Bible has the correct picture of God?

Well it's historically accurate, and there's prophecy and people are changed by it.

Don't psychologists sometimes get the same results?

No, it's different . . . .

But how exactly? It all depends on what you define as man's needs.

There are miracles, dramatic conversions . . . .

But there are moral people outside the church too.

Without the Bible there's no basis for morality.

65

There are all kinds of morality. How can you know which is the right one? How can you know anything?

You have to rely on . . . reason and . . .

Reason goes back to an assumption; it doesn't touch the real world.

I've heard so many great defenses of the faith.

What are the specifics?

The whole system hangs together. It offers so many wonderful answers.

Can man ever know anything as a certainty?

There's a lot of good evidence supporting the faith.

But isn't faith a leap in the dark?

I need a break.

But why don't you deal with it all the way through for once?

I'm not going to think about it for a while.

But you're thinking about not thinking about it.

No.

And now you're trying not to think about not thinking about it.

My head was spinning. I looked over at Henry, still poring over organic chemistry. He wouldn't understand. There were no shades of gray on the Kansas farm where he came from.

For months this voice of doubt had been slipping in to ambush my serenity. It was becoming more persistent, shadowing me like some faceless detective, always asking pointed questions, never letting me really answer. It kept poking around for some loophole in my faith, always insinuating there was a fatal flaw somewhere. I just couldn't come up with a coherent defense all the time.

Now I was going in circles, and the circles were tightening. I had never been so lost before in the disorder of my thoughts. The detective of doubt had me running scared.

The bell rang; time to get ready for bed. As I fumbled for my toothbrush and looked in the mirror, I realized that my problem had become more than philosophical musing. This was more like an attack on my mind. I couldn't think straight while pressed up against the wall and frisked for "five good reasons."

But climbing into bed I still wondered, was this something

unhealthy or was I just being unsparingly honest with my beliefs? As I stared at the dim ceiling in the heavy silence of the night, I felt terribly vulnerable.

Morning brought a cheerfully blue sky and Dr. Brunt's "Life and Teachings of Jesus." Dr. Brunt had a lively way of making that life and those teachings accessible. It was always refreshing to get a strong dose of clear-headed Christianity.

The brightness of that class made me long for a clear answer to my detective problem. Maybe there *was* a way out of my mental rut, even if I couldn't explain it to anyone. The old adage about fasting and praying came to mind. Maybe that would work. I had never tried it before and I was certainly desperate enough.

The next Saturday, I skipped breakfast and knelt alone in my room. Burying my head in my hands, I leaned into the Lord hard: "You know what a mess I'm in. You know every blind alley I've been down in search of a clear mind. You are the One who put all the circuits together in my head. I need some rewiring. I need . . . I don't know exactly what. But I've got to get out from under this weight of doubt. It makes me see only the shadows, when I know that Your world is full of light and color. I believe You have an answer for me. You've had the right answers before."

I began looking through the Bible for some potent word that could unknot my chronic tangle of reasons and rebuttals. Many verses on faith caught my attention—". . . comes by hearing, and hearing by the word of God." Yes, I was listening as best I could. "Faith in His name." Yes, I was concentrating on Christ.

I read about the peace that passes all understanding, about setting our hearts and minds on things above and bringing every thought into captivity to Christ.

Rebounding between Scripture and prayer, I kept after my goal. Paul's metaphor rang true. We *are* runners racing for a prize; we must persevere. It was all a matter of opening myself up to the Lord and hanging in there until something happened.

Only nothing happened. I was warmed and encouraged by the Word, but no clear answer popped out from its pages. I still had no alibi for my persistent detective.

In the afternoon I ran out of things to say to the Lord and decided to go out with a student "Sunshine Band" to a local hospital. For some reason, I felt benevolent after pleading with the Lord all morning on an empty stomach. And besides, it was a beautiful day.

Our van pulled up beside a large medical complex. I had never been inside before. As we passed through several hallways, the ubiquitous smell of medicine made me uneasy. Dull green tile echoed our footsteps. We glimpsed trays of stainless steel instruments in several rooms.

Finally we entered a post-operative ward to speak our dutifully cheerful words. One elderly gentleman thrashed and moaned on his bed. I expected his seizure to stop after a while. But it didn't. That was evidently his permanent condition. It was more than I could take in.

The room smelled of blood and urine. I began feeling a bit light-headed. I passed the bed of a young man stiffened in traction and then stopped to speak with another youth lying in sweat-soaked sheets. I couldn't keep my eyes off all the tubes attached to his body—a catheter, IV in his arm, and noisy oxygen tube through his nose. Feeling like I was going to pass out, I extended a few feeble words of encouragement, hurried back out to the van and collapsed on its carpeted floor.

I lay there regaining my strength, unsettled by the suffering I had seen up-close. I watched a few slow clouds through the windows. Then, out of the blue, something struck me: "It's only a feeling." That thought reverberated right through me.

Yes, that's exactly right. It *is* only a feeling. All this hide-and-seek game of apologetics has been so disturbing because it's been so vague. It has little to do with the content of faith. It's just an altercation of feelings.

That explanation seemed perfectly obvious. Surely it had occurred to me before. Despite all my previous efforts, however, I had been unable to stop fretting with the detective.

But lying in that van, the message—"it's only a feeling"—had the freeing power of a precise exorcism; the demon had been expelled. Everything cleared. I was not in the same mental impasse and I knew it.

The answer came so easily, and yet a long struggle preceded it. I had to become openly helpless before God—like those hospital patients, sweating and thrashing with their acute ailments.

I was never again subject to the introverted harassment of doubt. Although apologetics still interested me, I was no longer intimidated by mere shadows; I could face the issues.

Some time after that liberating experience, I asked the Lord to give me an extended rest from "defending the faith." I wanted to concentrate on other things besides apologetics and gave the whole weighty matter up into His hands.

At the end of that mental sabbatical, I discovered Francis Schaeffer's books. I had never imagined a Christian could so thoroughly deal with every aspect of thought and culture. Schaeffer put it all together in a biblical perspective. His aggressive apologetic swept me off my feet. I finally knew why the content of our faith is so coherent and well-grounded.

Through all this, God showed me His perfect timing. After I turned my thorny problems over to Him, He gave me clear answers on both an experiential and intellectual level—far better answers than I had thought possible.

My people, what have I done to you? How have I burdened you? Answer
me.

—Hosea 6:3, NIV.

Chapter 13

Without Premonition

Katey was a walking contradiction. Her obese body seemed
incapable of housing anything but jolly extroversion, yet inside
it, there lived a perceptive, sensitive spirit. Most people couldn't
get past the contradiction. Katey was clearly out of the social
mainstream at our Christian high school. But her friends knew
there was much more to Katey than flab.

I was fortunate to be one of them. Our friendship formed a
little island in the sea of post-adolescent dating games. I had no
need to flirt or show-off with Katey. Neither of us had to impress
the other. We were just friends.

Only Katey understood the long disjointed poems I wrote
secretly in my dormitory room. (What would the guys on my football team think?) She had a sympathetic imagination. We could
talk about images and dreams.

But Katey did not share my faith. She believed God hadn't
come around for her somehow, and only acknowledged Him from
a distance. For Katey, the good news about Christ meant only
boring chapel speeches.

And my friend had her list of grievances—The tragic death
of her roommate's father; hypocrisy among our Christian
teachers; the long catalog of petty rules trying in vain to define
religion for restive teenagers. Katey felt confined by it all.

I wanted her to see that Christ Himself is a live option, not
bound by the school's imperfections. She listened sympatheti-
cally but couldn't quite take the step of faith.

Shortly before graduation, Katey and some friends decided to celebrate their impending release with an evening excursion into town. Sneaking off campus at night was frowned upon in the school rule book. So when a faculty member spotted their car coasting into the girls' dorm parking lot at midnight, the dean was informed. After an interrogation, Katey received a summons to visit Mr. Ballinger, the principal.

This man possessed for us an almost mythical stature. Each day after assembly he would stand ramrod straight in front of the auditorium, dismissing the students by rows. His thick eyebrows and heavy jaw suggested the countenance of a displeased Old Testament prophet.

Mr. Ballinger had good intentions. He was not unkind. But he seemed aloof, and his bearing inspired fear and dislike among the students.

Katey was sure her appointment with the principal would mean the end—expulsion! In her mind, entry into his office spelled certain doom. Within his chamber the guilty pled in vain.

"I've already been in trouble this year," she told me. "This is it, Steve. Oh, I wanted to graduate so bad."

"You really think you'll be kicked out?" I asked.

"Yeah." She sounded resigned to her fate.

"Well then, why don't we ask God for help; see what He can do?"

"I don't know. This is really serious. I'm really in trouble."

"So, give Him a chance. Please."

Finally Katey agreed, as a last resort, to send up a humble petition that evening. I prayed hard that God would show Himself to the girl.

The following day Katey rushed into the library where I was studying. She whispered excitedly, "I don't believe it. He just told me not to go out again at night without permission. He gave me a warning—and that was it. I mean, I wasn't even grounded or anything."

"See what happens, Katey? God rides to the rescue. He really is interested in you. God wants to help you. He's not some stern judge up there waiting to catch you red-handed."

"Yeah, a lot of weird things have been happening to me lately. Like premonitions, you know. I've been reading about ESP. That stuff's really something."

"Katey, what does ESP have to do with it? We prayed to God and He answered us."

She acknowledged my point, but kept talking about the mysteries of psychic phenomena. "People have seen objects from thousands of miles away. . . ."

I realized the blow of grace had been dulled. It glanced off the dazzle of extra-sensory perception and her new "premonitions."

After graduation, during a summer trip, I stopped by Katey's home and met her parents. Katey's mother was tepidly religious. Her father, whom she adored, was not at all. Katey wondered out loud, "Is Dad going to be kept out of heaven? I don't know anyone else as kind."

The night before I left, we walked out by a neighborhood lake. The water rippled in moonlight. Scattered stars hinted at an awesome universe. We talked about our plans and tried to imagine where we would be in five years, or ten.

I wanted her to travel with Jesus. At times she seemed so close to dropping into His grasp. Her ideals; her commitment to true friendship made her vulnerable to His claims. Out there pacing on the lake shore, she did want to find out the meaning of it all. But something held Katey back—a deep sadness evident in her eyes. She wouldn't let go of it. She wanted God to say Sorry first.

So we went our separate ways. Katey studied nursing in Tennessee. I discovered the life of discipleship with Campus Crusade. It was refreshing to be part of a movement challenging the status quo of a secular university.

Three years later, Katey and I found ourselves at the same Michigan college. We had a lot to catch up on. She was still sensitive, but with a touch of bitterness. Most of her friends were Christian drop-outs, calloused to the "same old story of Jesus and His love." Katey did not share their cynical embrace of all things irreligious, but . . . sympathized.

And Katey had a boyfriend, George. They were meandering toward marriage.

I had one more chance to share with Katey. She let me use

her apartment to shoot some scenes for a film class. After the filming we began talking about the old days. In retrospect, she noticed the good times. Some of those school rules weren't so bad after all. Katey seemed to be reaching toward God.

"When are you going to decide, Katey?" I asked.

"I want to. But . . . I just can't."

I shared some of the practical things I had learned about the Christian life. If only she could catch the excitement . . . "I've seen all kinds of people changed. Christ is what's happening right now. It's beautiful to see lives turn around."

She was silent.

"Katey, are His terms too hard? All He asks us to do is accept His gift. It doesn't have to be a legalistic trip. Christ offers exactly what you're after. Why is it so difficult?"

Katey couldn't put her answer into words. That same undecipherable disappointment hung over her. She wouldn't let it go.

It was our last real conversation. We continued to say "hi" at the student center, and I got to know her fiancé, but I never touched Katey's inner thoughts again.

We graduated together for the second time, wished each other the very best, and went off to tackle the world in our different ways.

A few months later the shocking news came. George and Katey were out driving late one night. A drunk driver smashed through the freeway divider and collided head-on with their car. George was only shaken up. Katey died instantly.

Just like that. Still sensitive, only at the beginning . . . but everything ended.

Why? Why was it so hard to give Christ a chance? That question still haunts me.

I hope and pray that Katey broke through her sullen distance from grace before the end. But in this life, I will always feel the weight of her final disappointment, caught in mid-stride—without premonition.

I have drawn you with loving-kindness.

—Jeremiah 31:3, NIV.

Chapter 14

Unpromising Canvases

Gravel crackled under the tires as Nabe coasted up to his small two-story home. In the quiet of the night the car door slammed. The young man climbed his porch stairs carrying under his arm three large canvases.

Inside, his wife Yuki waited, rocking a baby in her dimly lit kitchen. Nabe mumbled a greeting but did not look at her as he set his canvases in a hallway closet.

Yuki laid the baby in its crib and heated up some tea. She fumbled with a scoop in the rice cooker and with difficulty spooned white grains into a glazed bowl. Shuffling into the living room she knelt beside her husband and carefully set rice, seaweed, and tea on a low table. Without speaking she moved slowly back into the kitchen.

As Yuki began rinsing dishes Nabe asked, "How were the kids?"

"All right," she replied, her voice trembling.

After a long pause Nabe spoke, "OK, so I was late this . . ."

"It's twelve-thirty," Yuki interrupted.

Nabe went on, "You've got to understand. It takes a lot of work to get anywhere in the art world."

"*I've* got to understand?" Yuki burst out. "You leave me alone with the children every night when I can hardly . . ." She shook her gnarled knuckles at her husband, tears spilling down her cheeks, "Don't you *see*? You never give a thought to how hard it is for us. You're always off in your crazy dream world."

Nabe looked down. "When we were first married you told me you liked my abstract paintings. You even encouraged me."

"Yes, you were full of promises then—fame and independence, a nice big house. Just wait a few years you said. Well I've waited too long. All I get is the pain."

"Yuki, listen to me. A man has got to pursue something with his life. If he doesn't have a dream he might as well be dead."

"We're already dead as far as you're concerned. This house is like a tomb."

Nabe grimaced and shook his head. He rose quickly from the table, spilling his tea, and walked out to the balcony for some cool air.

As soon as Nabe passed through the massive wooden gates of Ryoan Zen temple he felt different. It was always like that. The hassles of life seemed to dissolve as he walked by the stone garden with its quiet stream and ancient statues. The quotas and accounts at the pipe factory where he worked faded into insignificance.

Nabe bowed low in greeting before his teacher-priest and exchanged a few polite remarks about the blooming cherry trees. Slipping into a dark robe he entered a small room sided by classical wall paintings of the gods and sliding paper doors. Nabe crossed his legs on the *tatami* straw mats and became perfectly still.

But before he could empty his mind for *zen* meditation, a flood of turbulent thoughts rushed in for attention. There were so many conflicts in his life he couldn't resolve or escape. Even "Gutai," the avant-garde art group to which he belonged, had problems. It had started out so well—everyone full of ideals and enthusiasm for the artistic life. They had disdained the competition and pettiness of the "normal" business world.

But now the same dog-eat-dog mentality had infected the group. Some of the artists were selling, some weren't. Nabe had begun to notice jealousy and backbiting—all the things they had sought to escape in art. There seemed no way out of the dark side of human nature.

And then there was Yuki. It was hard to watch her slowly contort with arthritis. He felt terribly guilty about leaving her and the children alone so often. But how could he give up the only significant thing in his life? Nabe's whole mind and heart were compressed into the tableaus of dense geometry he painted. He longed to make history with his canvases.

Why did life always get twisted in such knots? Why did someone always have to suffer?

Nabe hoped Zen Buddhism would provide some answers. If only he could have that peace he had seen in the eyes of those few priests who had attained *satori*—enlightenment. Nabe shook his head and tried to concentrate again on the "perfect whiteness."

After a few minutes of mandarin oranges, rice crackers and small talk, Perry's study group settled into two sofas and opened their Bibles. Perry began to talk about the parable of the prodigal son. Nabe listened and watched intently as the young missionary's hands grew animated and his eyes sparkled. Perry's face was always so transparently eager when he spoke about the Gospel.

That was what had attracted Nabe in the beginning. He had first met Perry at an English school where he was studying the "international language" so he could communicate with the foreign artists and critics who came to see "Gutai." Something about the Canadian teacher struck Nabe as soon as he walked into the classroom. It was just a subjective impression, but the look on that nineteen-year-old kid's face seemed like the serene countenance of enlightened priests. And it had taken them decades to achieve it. Nabe had even heard of some priests who committed suicide because they failed to reach *satori* after 30 years of *zen* meditation.

Nabe had not been interested in attending Bible class when other teachers invited him. After all, he was an Eastern man; he had to pursue truth in an Eastern way. But Perry fascinated him. Nabe had decided to check out his Bible class just to see what made him tick.

At first he understood nothing. The God of the Bible was a mystifying stranger. Then he began to notice parallels to Zen thought in Scripture—the "all is vanity" in Ecclesiastes for example.

More recently, Nabe had come to understand something of the uniqueness of Christ. Perhaps He *was* the Man for humanity. Really, who could resist such a character? Jesus made an art out of life itself. His blank canvases were blind eyes, crippled limbs, and hard hearts. With a single word or touch He created beautiful new images.

As Perry expounded on the prodigal son and the father's unconditional love, a lot began to click in Nabe's mind—Christ's sacrifice, the solution to that dark side of human nature—being born again. It certainly seemed like God's kind of love was what he and his family desperately needed.

Nabe slid open the bedroom closet door, folded up two *futon* mattresses and shoved them into the shelves. He began vacuuming the smooth *tatami* mats. Yuki was out in a nearby park with the kids. Nabe had decided to clean up. It wasn't half bad really. Being a good husband and father mattered more than he had realized.

Just the other day Juki had said how surprised she was at the change in him. Nabe wasn't that aware of it, but his wife said he was much more considerate. He *was* aware that she listened now when he talked with her about things he was learning from the Bible.

After vacuuming the house, Nabe reached into the closet shelf for the *futons*. He felt something hard beneath them and pulled out a small red notebook. Curious, he leafed through it and recognized Yuki's handwriting. It was her diary, containing entries for the last several years. His name kept popping out from the lavender pages.

Nabe read about himself for hours in that quiet, empty bedroom. He couldn't stop. By the time the sun had brushed against trees on the horizon, tears were flooding down his cheeks. He saw what it was like to have to live with someone like himself. It looked so different from the other side—an endless corridor of pain, thoughts of suicide. All the ugliness of his selfish life swept over him like paint smearing together, blotting out a composition. And for the first time Nabe accepted it.

He stared out the window with the diary in his lap, remembering scenes that had only half registered before, until his children's voices filtered up from the driveway.

A large van pulled up and stopped beside two oaks and a quiet stream. Nabe stepped out and looked around. A trail led up a hill to a grassy, level spot surrounded by pines. Perfect spot for a picnic. He climbed on top of the van and began handing down wheelchairs to several assistants. They helped about a dozen youth into the chairs and then everyone moved slowly up the trail.

An amiable breeze rustled through the leaves and brushed against their faces. A couple of birds kept up a cheerful dialogue. Sunshine filled the glen with bright greens and deep shadows.

Nabe breathed deeply of the crisp air. This was the life. It was always exciting to see the faces of the handicapped light up when they were brought out into God's world. His "Helping Hand" project had created a lot more joy than he'd bargained for.

Nabe and Yuki had begun the ministry less than a year after their baptism. They had both been won by the boundlessness of God's love. Now they wanted to share it with those stuck in the "unsightly" corners of society.

In the pine-enclosed clearing Yuki began fixing lunch. Several of the fellows played a modified version of baseball. Nabe's two kids ran happily among the wheelchairs.

Nabe looked around at all the sunny faces. These people, too, were the objects of God's handiwork and the targets of His grace. Each one had broken through his or her physical restriction in some way—like the spastic kid who pitched with amazing accuracy. After each convoluted windup the ball somehow found the strike zone. Every person there embodied the promise of re-creation, of transcending the distortions that sin has intruded into the world.

The truth which Nabe had tried so hard to find in abstract designs and strong colors, now cried out in the lucent eyes around him. Here was all he had attempted to create on canvas—spiritual beauty in the superficially unattractive, a winning grace in the harsh angles of disabled limbs.

God would work His wonders on these unpromising, overlooked canvases. And Nabe was part of His artistry. Bursts of laughter existed now where there was lonely silence before, uninhibited play beneath a wide sky where there had been only cramped suffering.

Nabe looked over to see his wife stirring a large pot of stew, her face animated in conversation. Their eyes met. Yes, this was art they could both understand.

Behold the manner of love the Father has bestowed on us.

—1 John 3:1, NKJV.

Chapter 15

Night Watch

Jerry and I walk hurriedly into room 311 at the worst time. Barbara is trying to suction Dad, holding his restless tongue flat with a tongue depressor, wiggling the tube gingerly down his congested throat.

"If only I could keep him suctioned for one day," she explains reflexively, "maybe the pneumonia . . ." She pauses to greet us and thank Jerry and me for flying in from California. Her drawn face makes it clear she's been fighting a losing battle for some time.

I had come with anxious expectations. After the stroke, how pale and emaciated would his face be? I did not want to see those familiar, ruddy features wasting away. But it isn't his face, still holding a bit of color, that shocks. It's his terrible struggle for breath, chest and abdomen heaving, never a moment's rest. I wasn't ready for this kind of suffering.

Then Barbara breaks down. The frustration of struggling alone is too much. She'd promised herself she wasn't going to cry, but helpless, grateful tears well up in her eyes. So Jerry and I, white-faced, jump into the fray. Trembling, we try to get the tube down deeper in order to suction out the deadly, ever-forming mucus and watch his eyes roll and his head shake in vain. His limbs are weak, his moans strong.

It is Saturday morning, a cold autumn day in Illinois. Jerry has to go to the airport in Moline to pick up Dan, who's flying in from Colorado. Outside the room Jerry begins weeping uncon-

6—T.F.

trollably. He continues sobbing on the interstate past miles of broad, flat farmland full of dead leaves.

Jerry remembers. Dad had been a man of few fears. We three boys grew up under the umbrella of his steadfast moral courage. But he had expressed one apprehension: he didn't want to die in a hospital—life taken away in small clinical pieces. Jerry remembers and weeps.

Back in 311 Barbara talks to Dad incessantly. She wipes his forehead, smooths the sheets, suctions, adjusts the oxygen tube, and pours out hopeful, devoted words on her husband of three months. Every groan becomes a sentence she completes. She repeats his name, nods yes, yes, encourages every breath. By sheer force of will she creates conversation in that brain flooded with sinister blood.

But I grow weary with the struggle and imagine Dad is too. If only he could sleep a little.

Barbara says the doctor has left floor nurses instructions not to resuscitate Dad should he stop breathing. I want to know why.

Out in the hall the doctor outlines the damage caused by a ruptured artery in the brain.

"So what are his chances of recovering?"

"I would say almost none."

"You're saying his brain is dead?"

"Well, even if he recovers from the pneumonia, you have to think of what you are going to have left. In order to recover, your father must regain basic functions. He must be able to swallow, to eat, he must be truly alert, recognize people. Otherwise he will just be a vegetable, I'm afraid."

"What about words—talking? Barbara has heard him say a few."

"Well, on occasion a patient may say a word, or move a limb, but it could just be reflex action; it doesn't really mean the brain is functioning adequately."

I still wanted to know how the doctor was making his evaluation: "OK, you did a brain scan. Can you tell exactly how and where the brain is damaged?"

"Well, a brain scan doesn't really tell you about the future. Some people with minor damage will never recover; others with half their brains gone function normally. The key is still function—the ability to eat and be alert."

The doctor leaves us with the suggestion that at some point the family might start thinking about when it would be appropriate to stop artificial support systems.

So we stand numbly in the hallway as visitors walk by. Their footsteps on the hard tiles echo harshly across the bare beige walls. Finally Barbara sobs, "I just wish I could have known him longer." I embrace her awkwardly and think, yeah that's the rub, three months together and zap. I mumble a few words about heaven. It is the first time in my life I have referred to it as a present consideration.

For some reason the hospital attendants move Dad to room 309. I can't decide whether that's good or bad. After he's settled in, Barbara wipes his forehead, smooths the sheets, suctions, adjusts the oxygen tube, and pours out her hopeful devoted words. She tells me the pastor plans to be here at 3:00 for an anointing service.

I wonder how I should pray. It seems to me that an "if-it-be-thy-will" petition is very near to no petition at all. I'm quite willing to wield some hard-hitting promises and pound on heaven's door like that persistent widow in Jesus' parable. But I don't want to see Dad go on suffering pointlessly. I'm also willing to cooperate passively and give him up into God's hands. Should I fight in petition or should I rest in submission?

For some reason, looking at Dad's heaving thorax in room 309, I'm not willing to settle for a safe medium. I want his condition to go one way or the other. After praying about how to pray, I recall the doctor's words concerning function. Maybe that could be a sign. We could ask God to give us an indication about how He wants us to pray—and it wouldn't be something arbitrary.

Yes, there are two specific things: swallowing and recognizing people. If we see some bit of progress in these areas then we will know we should petition for recovery all the way in earnest. If not, we will rest in prayer.

Barbara and I have a long talk about this and we agree that our part in the anointing will be to ask for these particular signs.

The pastor and an elder arrive—old friends of the family. The pastor takes out his tiny bottle of oil and rubs a little on Dad's furrowed forehead. He places a hand on Dad's numb shoulder and begins to pray quietly. It is a very mild petition, just laying things out before the will of the Lord.

Suddenly, Dan walks in the room, the first-born, tall and broad-shouldered. Everyone looks up and sees his face is white as a sheet. He strides over to the bed, bends down to kiss Dad and says, "I love you."

It turns out he and Jerry walked into room 311 and found an empty bed, newly made. For a moment Dan thought he had arrived too late. After the relief of finding the right room, he wanted to make sure he got the good word in.

There are polite hugs all around, clumsy words of encouragement for all present. Jerry and Dan say they will stay with Dad and tell me to go out for some food. I persuade Barbara to take a break too.

Driving up the gravel road to Dad and Barbara's country house I spot the red barn he had built for his horses.

While Barbara fixes a bite I walk over to take a look. Beneath a covering of leaves, the grass looks terribly green, green as the tall stands I've seen at Dad's boyhood farm near Texarcana. I step inside the barn and smell the pungent hay. The horses are gone. But every beam stands sturdy as ever. Solid oak. He put up most of it by himself.

Dad built well. I remember all the times I relied on him. I remember when I was five. Slipped off his back while he was climbing out of the swimming pool. I couldn't swim, but they say I just lay in the water calmly sinking, sure that Dad would fetch me out again—and of course he did.

I was twelve, walking with him in the woods he loved. It was always easy to talk. I had so many questions about right and wrong. And he lived the answers.

I was twenty, coming home from college on vacation. We would sit out on the porch looking at sunset. And when I shared how my faith was growing, his eyes would sparkle.

It is getting late. Shadows settle over the cornfields bordering Dad's place. I take a last look up at the sturdy oak rafters, breathe deeply the fragrance of wood and hay, and walk out into the dusk, very grateful for good shelter.

Back at the hospital Jerry and Dan report that Dad has slept awhile, breathing rather restfully for the first time. It is exhilarating news.

That night the three of us keep a vigil in room 309, watching over the helpless man who changed our diapers. He still heaves sometimes, but is definitely sleeping more than struggling. On occasion he snoozes very quietly. His shallow, but regular breathing sounds wonderful.

We don't talk much, mainly play an extended version of the five-letter-word game. But our night watch feels good. We change his position at regular intervals, fiddle with the blankets and jump up whenever he groans.

Slowly I begin to understand why Dad always got up around 2:00 a.m. to check on us and smooth our blankets—even after we were older. This is the only time we have been up in the night for the one who was up so many nights for us. This is unexplored territory. In its strange stillness I come face to face with the power of his love for me. And I know now that I will love my children with the same unquenchable desire.

About ten o'clock Sunday morning, Dan, Jerry, and I return to the hospital after a few hours of sleep. Nurses have disconnected the oxygen. Dad is breathing just fine on his own. They think he's licked the pneumonia. One of them says, "A miracle is just what we needed around here."

I walk over to the bed, Dad sees me and smiles. I grab onto the faint twinkle in his eyes for all I'm worth. A good sign. Then he asks for water. I hold a paper cup to his lips, he gulps, and swallows, yes swallows twice. We're jubilant. Two signs. I remember that I can pound on heaven's door now without reservation. But of course I've jumped the gun and have already been petitioning very pointedly.

We spend the day congratulating Dad on his imminent recovery and exercising the languid limbs on his paralyzed right side. Each of us spot more signs of recognition in his eyes. That night my brothers and I take turns keeping watch at the hospital. Dad sleeps like a baby.

Monday it's time to fly back to our other homes. Dad is making gains by the hour. We say goodbye in good spirits. At the airport the three of us remind each other how fortunate it was we arrived right at the critical time. We were glad we were there to witness and participate. Our farewell embraces are strong and sure, no longer those of awkward, self-conscious children. We clutch at roots, almost torn up, that now bind us more visibly together within the miracle of a Father's love.

Chapter 16

I Am Thirsty

With a quick rebuke the stormy sea calms down like a naughty child brought suddenly to its senses. With another unassuming phrase the rotting flesh of a leper is fired to ruddy health. An outstretched hand extinguishes somehow the madness of men made demons.

With good reason we don't usually think of Christ as a man needing any favors. His is the figure of a savior completely in control of every situation. Out of His inexhaustible abundance He freely gave.

And yet, as One who took on the frailties of the flesh, He certainly was in need. Jesus grew weary, thirsty, and hungry. He experienced disappointment and coveted human sympathy.

If we look carefully, one of the most enlightening portraits to emerge out of the rich imagery of the Gospels is a picture of Jesus as a man asking others for a favor. There is much more than first meets the eye or ear in Christ's simple requests. They illuminate the skillful grace that motivated His entire ministry.

It is high noon. Jesus has been walking through the Palestinian heat for several hours. Finally He arrives at Jacob's Well. At times like this the thought of a cool drought is enough to drive everything else from a man's head.

A Samaritan woman is drawing up her bucket and Jesus asks, "Will you give me a drink?" The woman is surprised that this Jewish stranger would ask a drink from a despised Samaritan.

Jesus takes the opportunity to turn her attention to the "living water" He can bestow.

Through one simple act of asking a stranger for a drink Jesus sets in motion a series of responses that will bring this Samaritan woman to a knowledge of salvation. The Master broke through centuries of racial and religious prejudice, not being condescending, but by placing Himself in debt—a debt He soon repays with considerable interest.

At first the woman can only understand the "spring of water welling up to eternal life" in terms of a labor-saving device: "Sir, give me this water so that I won't get thirsty and have to keep coming here to draw water." See John 4:15. But then Jesus starts getting personal. He gently turns over the stained pages of her past. He refuses to be distracted by the thorny question of whether Jerusalem or Samaria is the true place of worship. And finally, He gets the woman to focus on the source of the "living water." She tells her neighbors, "Come, see a man who told me everything I ever did." Verse 29.

Christ's request for a drink provides the illustrative key that opens this woman's mind to grasp spiritual realities for the first time. The Galilean stranger makes immediate and tangible the gift that so many people pass by.

And so the small bucket lowered into Jacob's well ends up drawing a whole village to the stirring knowledge that this thirsty Man is indeed the Saviour of the world.

Jesus is on His way to Jerusalem. As He passes through Jericho, a large crowd lines the road, eager for a glimpse of the celebrated rabbi from Nazareth. Zacchaeus, the local tax-collector, stands among them on tiptoe. He is very wealthy and very short. Determined to see Jesus, he climbs a sycamore tree and joins the street urchins peering through the leaves.

Zacchaeus was not beloved in Jericho. The fact that he was soaking its citizens for taxes on behalf of the hated Romans put him pretty much in the mud at the bottom of the totem pole.

Like the Samaritan woman, Zacchaeus is a social outcast. But unlike her he has already begun to feel remorse over his indulgent life style. He is attracted by the selfless ministry of Christ and longs for some way to identify with Him.

Jesus approaches the sycamore tree, spots his man out on a limb, and says, "Zacchaeus, come down immediately. I must stay at your house today." Luke 19:5. Inviting yourself over for supper seems a bit forward even for a popular rabbi. But Christ has apprehended loneliness and hope in a human face, and He will not pass by.

Once again a simple request pulls the rug out from under the whole oppressive caste structure of society. As the walls of separation come tumbling down, the religious "pillars of society" are left gasping in the rubble. They mutter indignantly, "He has gone to be the guest of a sinner." Verse 7.

But for Zacchaeus this proves to be a blow of grace that brings him out of the tree and down on his knees in repentance. "Look, Lord!" he cries, "here and now I give half of my possessions to the poor." Verse 8. Zacchaeus gladly welcomes the One who has affirmed his secret longings by asking for a favor.

Two instances recorded in the Gospels depict Jesus soliciting something for His use. Before His triumphal entry into Jerusalem, He sends His disciples ahead to requisition a donkey and her colt. For the Last Supper, Jesus reserves a certain large upper room in the city.

In the triumphal entry Christ presents Himself to the people as their Messianic King. And at the Last Supper He offers Himself in symbols as the Passover Lamb. It is for man that He establishes His kingdom and it is for man that He lays Himself down as atoning sacrifice. And in these two events He asks ordinary people to play a part with Him.

Christ doesn't condescendingly nudge us into servility. He rides on our donkey and eats in our guest room. In arranging for this human assistance, Christ shows that we are not mere spectators but participants in the last climactic scenes of His life—participants in His kingdom and in His death. Our lives matter a great deal; they are bound up in the passion of Christ.

Gethsemane. The weight of the sins of the world is slowly crushing out the life of Christ. He sees clearly every detail of His coming ordeal on the cross. He will soon be stretched taut between heaven and earth, the ultimate outcast. But even more terrifying than the prospect of physical agony is Jesus' sense that the Father is tearing Himself away. That He cannot bear.

So He turns to His disciples and says, "My soul is overwhelmed with sorrow to the point of death. Stay here and keep watch with me." Matthew 26:38. Jesus' need for companionship is intense. If only a few other living souls would stay awake with Him as His grisly darkness descends. . . .

But three times during that long night Jesus rises from the hard, cold ground, moves over to His huddled disciples—and each time finds them slumbering. Christ's three closest friends snore through the whole ordeal.

It would have been so easy for Him to rebuke His groggy disciples: "For three years I poured my whole life into you, and now, the one time I really need you. . ." Instead He urges Peter, "Watch and pray so that you will not fall into temptation. The spirit is willing, but the body is weak." Verse 41, NIV. It is the disciples Jesus is thinking about. Even though He shudders at the epicenter of a cosmic conflict, Christ's concern centers on the trial His disciples are about to go through.

Again we see Christ's gracious intent behind His request. Keeping a vigil with Christ is the best way for the disciples to be strengthened—to stand when things start falling apart. Christ asks for the favor that would save them from failure.

Jesus is arrested, tried, and crucified. All through the mockery and the beatings He remains utterly isolated. When He next opens His lips to ask a favor, they are cracked and parched. As the Messiah's body is increasingly distended on the cross, He slowly suffocates. The thirst of a dying man is cruel. Christ's pain is as loud and persistent as any man's would be.

John remembered that his Lord cried out, "I am thirsty." But another fact also struck the apostle. Christ was silent about His need until the very end, until all was accomplished, before making a last request "that the Scripture would be fulfilled." John 19:28, NIV.

First and foremost in Christ's mind is His determination to

complete His atonement for man's sin. He is fulfilling a promise made long ago, repeated for generations in slain lambs and stone altars until this very moment.

Saving mankind remains Christ's burning desire. It is evident His spiritual thirst has not slaked since His early encounter with the woman at the well. At the cross we see that Christ's thirst for human beings overpowers even the loudest physical cravings. He longs to draw all people to Himself. The cross becomes a weapon wielded in the Messiah's hands. His cry pierces our hearts—*I am thirsty!*

A few days after burying their Lord, the disciples huddle behind locked doors. Their Master has been murdered. His cause seems lost. They wonder gloomily about their own fate.

Suddenly Jesus appears before them. The disciples think this is just too good to be true. They spring back as if looking at a ghost.

Jesus shows them His three-day-old wounds. "Look at my hands and my feet," He insists. "It is I myself! Touch me and see." Luke 24:39, NIV. But they can't quite grasp the fact that this figure before them is the same One they took down cold and broken from the cross.

As they stare benumbed, Jesus breaks the spell with a disarming request, Do you have anything here to eat?" Verse 41, NIV. They hand Him a piece of broiled fish, and as He sits down to eat, the reality of the resurrection is sealed in the minds of Christ's messengers.

"Then he opened their minds so they could understand the Scriptures." Verse 45, NIV. Jesus shows how the pieces of the drama—His life, death and resurrection—fit together. In the night following their Master's arrest the disciples had lost sight of His mission on earth. Now it is breathtakingly clear. Sitting there eating a piece of fish, Jesus is the exclamation point of His own exposition.

In asking others for a favor, Christ demonstrates His ingenious grace, a grace that stands in sharp contrast to our own pretensions to goodness. So often a self-serving angle lies embedded in our most generous acts. Jesus, on the other hand, invariably smuggles some essential blessing for the other into every favor He seeks.

Even as a worn-out traveler looking for a drink, or a dying rabbi desperate for companionship, Christ remains a gracious servant. His performance stands as the most unforgettable picture we posses of God's wondrous love.